cooking with

herbs & spices

cooking with
herbs & spices

Linda Tubby and
Manisha Gambhir Harkins
with photography by Peter Cassidy

RYLAND
PETERS
& SMALL
LONDON NEW YORK

Designer Iona Hoyle
Commissioning Editor Julia Charles
Editor Rachel Lawrence
Production Sheila Smith
Art Director Anne-Marie Bulat
Publishing Director Alison Starling

Food Stylist Linda Tubby
Prop Stylist Róisín Nield
Indexer Hilary Bird

First published in the United Kingdom in 2006
by Ryland Peters & Small
20–21 Jockey's Fields
London WC1R 4BW
www.rylandpeters.com

10 9 8 7 6 5 4 3 2 1

ISBN-10: 1 84597 231 7
ISBN-13: 978 1 84597 231 8

A CIP record for this book is available from the British Library.

Printed and bound in China

Notes

- All spoon measurements are level, unless otherwise specified.
- All eggs are medium, unless otherwise specified. Uncooked or partially cooked eggs should not be served to the very young, the very old, those with compromised immune systems or to pregnant women.
- Fresh herbs should be used, unless otherwise specified. If using dried herbs instead of fresh for any reason, use one-third of the quantity mentioned.
- Ingredients in this book are available from larger supermarkets, specialist greengrocers and Asian shops and markets. Some of the more unusual herbs must be sought out in garden centres or grown in your own garden. See pages 188–189 for mail order sources.
- Ovens should be preheated to the specified temperature. The majority of the recipes in this book were tested using a regular oven. If using a fan oven, cooking times and temperatures should be adjusted according to the manufacturer's instructions. Where a recipe has been tested in a fan oven, specific instructions are given in individual recipes.
- For all recipes requiring dough or batter, liquid measurements are given as a guide. Always add liquid gradually to achieve the desired consistency, rather than adding it all at once. Use your eyes and your sense of touch to achieve the best results. Remember that different flours vary in weight. For example, you will find that masa harina, buckwheat flour, rice flour and even wheat flours like superfine wholemeal, or fine-textured white bread flour can weigh less per volume than plain flour. If you don't use the flour specified in a recipe, the result may be affected.

Sterilization of preserving jars

- It is essential for health reasons that jars are sterilized before they are filled with jam or chutney.
- Wash the jars in hot, soapy water and rinse in boiling water. Put into a large saucepan and then cover with hot water. With the lid on, bring the water to the boil and continue boiling for 15 minutes. Turn off the heat, then leave the jars in the hot water until just before they are to be filled. Invert the jars onto a clean cloth to dry. Sterilize the lids by boiling for 5 minutes, or according to the manufacturer's instructions. The jars should be filled and sealed while they are still hot.

contents

introduction

Herbs and spices are an essential part of cooking all over the world. From the spice pastes of South-east Asia to the bouquet garni of French cuisine, they have long been used to enhance all kinds of sweet and savoury dishes.

Spices are the seeds, roots and rhizomes, barks, buds, stigmas or berries of certain plants and are often used in dried form. Herbs are the leaves and stalks of certain aromatic plants and are usually best used fresh. The same plant can occasionally be the source of a herb and a spice, of which coriander is a classic example.

Both herbs and spices have been around as a natural resource for thousands of years. Many herbs, such as basil, coriander, dill and parsley, were originally native to southern Europe and used by the Ancient Greeks and Romans for food, medicinal and ceremonial purposes. The Roman army made great use of herbs to nurture mind, body and spirit and took their herbs and spices with them as they rampaged their way across the known world. Until relatively recent times, herbs were the principle source of medicine available and were used to cure everything from toothache to liver disease.

Due to the ease with which they could be dried, spices were a valuable trade commodity in times past. Along with fabrics and precious metals, they were traded along the Silk Road, a series of trade routes stretching across Asia, for many centuries. When the Spanish conquistadors arrived in South America in the 15th century, they took with them many of the spices that were to become an integral part of Latin American cooking, including coriander, cumin and cinnamon. Spanish and Portuguese merchants transported chillies to Europe and to their colonies in Asia and Africa, from where they were exported to the Middle East and China. Chilli became a key crop in India (which has since become the world's biggest exporter of chillies) and it was also traded for cloves, nutmeg and mace from the Spice Islands of Indonesia.

Throughout history, recipes have been a product of whatever ingredients have been locally available and knowledge of herbs and spices has passed down from generation to generation. Certain combinations of herbs and spices have become integral to different cuisines, for example the lemongrass and ginger intrinsic to Thai cooking, the coriander and chilli used in Mexican salsas or the aromatic spice blends typical of North African cooking.

Whilst some herbs, such as thyme, tarragon, oregano and bay leaves, have specific uses in their dried forms, it is generally better to use fresh herbs and to buy them from a source with a fast turnover. Both dried herbs and spices lose pungency with age, so buy little and often.

There are literally hundreds of varieties of herbs that can be bought or grown, and the range of spices available is ever-increasing due to advances in production methods. With this rich and colourful palette of ingredients to choose from, cooking with herbs and spices has never been so inspiring and this book shows you how to make dishes from all over the world that are simply bursting with flavour.

herb tips

Choosing herbs Herbs are better value and have a better flavour if you buy them in big bunches from street markets and farmers' markets. Herbs bought in small packs or little pots from a supermarket may have been pampered in polytunnels and grown out of their natural season, so check their flavour. Each herb adds its own character of flavour and fragrance on a sliding scale. Some herbs can be quite overpowering if used in a heavy-handed way, so get to know their strength. The herb's aroma and flavour comes from the volatile oils stored in the leaves, flowers and stems. The time of day they are harvested and the seasons can have a marked effect on their strength. The same herb grown in a variety of conditions can smell and taste quite different. Woody herbs tend to stand up to longer cooking and can be added at the beginning of cooking. Those with soft leaves are a little more sensitive and are best added towards the end to retain their flavour and goodness.

Preserving herbs Once, dried herbs were almost the only preserved form available. Herbs grew in summer and were dried for use throughout the winter and early spring. Some kept their flavour – and even became stronger – while others faded. Modern farming methods allow us to buy many herbs at any time of year, but their flavour can be inferior. Herbs can be preserved in oil (page 170) or frozen and used straight from the freezer – many tropical herbs, such as lemongrass, kaffir lime leaves and curry leaves, benefit from this treatment. If using dried herbs, use a small quantity – no more than one-third of that given in the recipe. If you don't have a certain herb, you can often replace it with another – use your sense of smell and taste, and be creative.

Chopping and preparing herbs Herbs give out their individual aroma and flavour when chopped, shredded, torn, bruised, crushed or heated. Use a very sharp knife (or a mezzaluna) for chopping herbs. Wrap the herbs into a tight bunch, then chop with the blade close to your fingers, and angled away from you. Dry leaves are better to work with, so after washing, drain well and leave to dry on kitchen paper for 20 minutes, if possible.

spice tips

Buying spices If possible, buy whole spices and grind them yourself. They last much longer and you will know that they are fresh. However, most of us buy some ground spices for ease and 'ethnic' shops are a good source of these because they're less expensive and sell larger quantities than supermarkets. Take advantage where spices are sold loose, as this allows you to smell and judge whether they are fresh or old. Some commercially blended spices can be of good quality and can be handy for blends that include arcane spices. For the most part, however, it is always best to grind your own blends using a coffee grinder, blender or food processor.

Storing spices Store spices in airtight containers – glass bottles are perfect. Ground spices stored thus will last a few months; to keep them longer, refrigerate or freeze them. Some spices, like fresh ginger or galangal, won't keep for very long, so slice, seal and freeze them. To use, pour a little boiling water over a slice and leave for a few minutes. Lump tamarind keeps for a long time, while tamarind paste will have a use-by date on the bottle.

Bruising and toasting spices Some whole spices need to be bruised before use, to release aroma and flavour. Toasting spices is essential for many recipes and brings out the best flavour. Fry spices for just 1–2 minutes over low heat as they burn easily. You will smell their scent when they're ready. Let the spices cool and dry off before grinding.

Cooking with spices Whole spices can be added directly to stocks and soups or they can be fried ('tempered') in hot oil first. Ground spice mixtures can be added directly to a dish at different times: prior to cooking, as in a marinade, or a few minutes before a dish is served. Spice pastes can be simple or complex and are usually stir-fried in oil before other ingredients are added. Cook over low heat so that the paste doesn't burn and add a drop of water to stop it sticking, if necessary. For best results, follow these general rules as well as individual recipe methods.

soups & salads

- tarragon
- flat leaf parsley
- basil
- marjoram
- Chinese flowering chives (kuchai; left)

herb and carrot soup

3 thin leeks, thinly sliced
2 garlic cloves, crushed
1 tablespoon sunflower oil
600 g young carrots, well scrubbed and thinly sliced
1.2 litres vegetable stock or water
40 g bunch of sorrel, stalks removed and leaves chopped
leaves from 4 sprigs of tarragon
leaves from 6 sprigs of flat leaf parsley
leaves from 4 sprigs of basil
leaves from 6 sprigs of marjoram

to serve

100 ml crème fraîche
12 bocconcini, torn in half, or 2 regular mozzarella cheeses, torn into pieces
a handful of Chinese flowering chives (kuchai), or regular chives
freshly ground black pepper

serves 6

Aromatherapy in a soup – this dish tastes marvellous, and if you're able to grow all the ingredients yourself, you'll feel wonderfully virtuous. Purée the soup coarsely, so that the brilliant carrot orange is just flecked with green. The *bocconcini* – little mouthfuls of mozzarella – peep out from just under the surface. Sprinkle with Chinese flowering chives if you have them, otherwise regular chives will taste good, too.

Put the leeks, garlic and oil in a small saucepan, cover with a lid and cook gently for 5 minutes. Add the carrots and cook gently for a further 5 minutes. Add the stock, bring to the boil and simmer for 5 minutes. Lower the heat, add the sorrel and simmer, uncovered, for a further 5 minutes.

Coarsely chop the tarragon, parsley, basil and marjoram. Stir into the soup. Strain the mixture through a sieve into a clean saucepan and put the solids into a food processor or blender with a little of the liquid. Blend to a coarse purée, then return to the saucepan and reheat.

Remove from the heat and fold in the crème fraîche. Ladle into hot bowls and add a few bocconcini pieces to each one. Sprinkle with chive flowers and black pepper, then serve.

- kaffir lime leaves
- ginger (left)
- chilli
- flat Chinese chives
- Thai sweet basil

thai lobster noodle soup

Like so much Thai food, this recipe has a delicate balance of spicy, fresh, zesty flavours. Kaffir lime leaves are now widely available, either as part of a Thai flavour pack in supermarkets, or in big bags from Asian or Chinatown markets. Buy the whole bag and freeze them, then use straight from frozen. Ginger can also be frozen, then grated straight from the freezer. Both flavours contrast well with the richness of the coconut cream and lobster. Although less Thai than Japanese, seaweed and sesame seeds make a delicious addition to this soup.

2 small cooked lobsters or crayfish tails, shells removed

120 g dried shrimp

3 kaffir lime leaves, torn

3 cm fresh ginger, peeled

200 g wide rice noodles (sen lek)

2 tablespoons hijiki seaweed

2 tablespoons mirin (sweetened Japanese rice wine)

200 ml coconut cream

2 tablespoons fish sauce

freshly squeezed juice of 1 lime

2 mild red chillies, halved lengthways, deseeded and thinly sliced into strips

2 mild green chillies, halved lengthways, deseeded and thinly sliced into strips

a handful of flat Chinese chives, sliced diagonally

75 g thin green beans, sliced in half lengthways and cooked

2 sprigs of Thai sweet basil (optional)

serves 4

Put the lobster shells, dried shrimp and kaffir lime leaves in a large saucepan. Add 1.5 litres water and bring to the boil, then lower the heat and simmer for 1 hour. Strain the stock, grate the ginger and squeeze the juice from it into the stock.

Soak the noodles in a bowl of cold water for 20 minutes. When soft, drain well and cover until needed. Put the seaweed in a bowl and stir in the mirin.

Add the coconut cream to the stock, stir well and bring to the boil. Lower the heat, then add fish sauce and lime juice to taste.

When ready to serve, add the drained noodles to the stock and reheat. Ladle into hot bowls, then add the chillies, Chinese chives, green beans and lobster meat. Drain the seaweed and sprinkle it over the soup, then top with Thai sweet basil leaves and serve.

Note Fishmongers and Chinese supermarkets often have frozen crayfish tails, which are good for this recipe. Instead of hijiki seaweed, you can use black sesame seeds to sprinkle on top of the soup.

- Cajun spice blend
- oregano

cajun-spiced chowder

with corn and bacon

4 ears of corn or 475 g fresh or frozen kernels

25 g butter

1 onion, finely chopped

1 small celery stalk, finely chopped

4–5 slices back bacon, chopped

1½ teaspoons Cajun Spice Blend (page 172), plus extra to garnish

1.25 litres vegetable stock

250 ml single cream

to serve

2 tablespoons freshly chopped oregano

crusty bread

green salad

serves 4

Chowders are creamy, chunky soups, the most famous of which is New England clam chowder. Corn chowders are popular too – a real taste of America. This version takes inspiration from the Deep South and the result is Louisiana soul food with just the right amount of Acadian (Cajun country) spice. Commercial Cajun spice blends are often a long way from their original form – some brands are not bad, while others add far too much cayenne, and sometimes totally unnecessary MSG. It is very easy to make your own blend – remembering that the three peppers (white, black and cayenne) are essential, when properly balanced, to the Cajun way of spicing. Celery salt is also part of the blend, so extra salt is not necessary.

If using fresh ears of corn, remove the husks and silks and cut the stalk end flat. Put the flat end on a board and cut off the kernels from top to bottom. Discard the cobs.

Melt the butter in a large saucepan, add the onion and sauté for 5 minutes. Add the celery and sauté for a further 3 minutes until well softened. Add the bacon and cook for 1–2 minutes. Add the corn and Cajun spice blend and mix well.

Add the vegetable stock and bring to the boil. Reduce the heat and simmer for about 35 minutes. Add the cream and simmer until thickened. You can serve the soup immediately or, to thicken it further, put a ladle of the chowder (without any of the bacon) into a food processor or blender and purée until smooth. Pour the blended chowder back into the saucepan and mix well.

To serve, ladle into bowls and top with a little oregano and a very light dusting of Cajun spice blend. Serve hot with crusty bread and a green salad.

- bay leaf
- black pepper
- allspice

butternut squash soup

with allspice and pine nuts

1 medium butternut squash, halved lengthways and deseeded

25 g unsalted butter

1 large leek, trimmed and chopped

1 bay leaf

a few black peppercorns, crushed

4–5 allspice berries, crushed

600 ml vegetable stock

60 g pine nuts, toasted in a dry frying pan, plus extra to serve (optional)

crusty bread, to serve

a non-stick baking sheet

serves 4

This is a quintessentially American soup, which is popular in both northern and southern states. Squashes and allspice are native to the Americas and pine nuts have been gathered in the deserts of the South-west for at least a thousand years. The key to this soup is the light spicing and the roasting of the butternut squash to bring out the best of its sweet flavour.

Put the butternut squash halves flesh side down onto the baking sheet. Roast in a preheated fan oven at 190°C (375°F) Gas 5 for 45 minutes or until tender. (If using a regular oven, adjust the cooking time and temperature according to the manufacturer's instructions.) Remove from the oven and, using a spoon, scoop the flesh out of the skins into a bowl. Discard the skins.

Put the butter into a large saucepan and melt over medium to low heat. Add the leek, bay leaf, peppercorns and allspice and fry gently until the leek begins to soften. Add the butternut squash, stock and 1 litre water. Bring to the boil, reduce the heat and simmer for about 10 minutes, or until the leeks are very soft.

Remove the bay leaf and transfer the soup to a food processor or blender. Add the pine nuts and blend until smooth, working in batches if necessary. Return the soup to the saucepan and reheat. Serve hot with crusty bread and sprinkled with toasted pine nuts, if liked.

- garlic
- hot pimentón
- saffron (left)

andalusian chickpea soup

with chorizo, paprika and saffron

2 tablespoons extra virgin olive oil

1 onion, chopped

3 thin celery stalks, chopped, with leaves reserved

1 large carrot, chopped

2 garlic cloves, chopped

250 g chorizo, skinned, halved, then cut into 1-cm slices (or a mixture of chorizo and another Southern European sausage, such as morcilla or fresh small salami)

400 g canned chickpeas, drained

1.75 litres chicken stock

¼ teaspoon hot pimentón (Spanish oak-smoked paprika)

125 g spinach, tough stalks removed and leaves coarsely chopped into large pieces

¼ teaspoon saffron threads, bruised with a mortar and pestle

to serve

Manchego or Parmesan cheese, shaved (optional)

crusty bread (optional)

serves 4

This hearty soup is a meal in itself. Chunks of chorizo, and perhaps morcilla (black pudding) or other sausages, float alongside chickpeas and spinach in a slightly smoky, fragrant broth. The special flavour comes from two typically Spanish spices, pimentón (Spanish oak-smoked paprika, made from a variety of capsicum or pepper) and its home-grown luxury spice, saffron. Although saffron is grown in many parts of the world, from Kashmir to Turkey, it is said that the best comes from La Mancha in Central Spain.

Heat the olive oil in a large saucepan and add the onion, celery and carrot. Gently sauté the vegetables until they begin to soften. Add the garlic, chorizo, chickpeas, stock and pimentón. Bring to the boil, reduce the heat and simmer for about 10 minutes. Add the spinach and celery leaves and simmer for a further 15 minutes.

Add the saffron and clean out the mortar using a little of the stock, so as not to waste any of the expensive saffron. Add to the saucepan and simmer for another 5 minutes. Serve hot in large, wide bowls as a main course lunch. Add shavings of cheese, if using. This soup is very filling, but some good crusty bread and perhaps some extra cheese make delightful partners.

• shichimi togarashi spice mix

miso and wakame soup
with japanese seven-spice

2 tablespoons dried wakame seaweed

3 tablespoons miso paste

125 g firm tofu, cut into 1-cm cubes

1 spring onion, trimmed and thinly sliced

Shichimi Togarashi (page 178) or ground sansho pepper, to serve

dashi*

1 piece dried kombu seaweed, 5 cm square

15 g dried bonito flakes (ana-katsuo), about 6 tablespoons

serves 4

Classic in its simplicity, miso soup warms and entices at the beginning of a Japanese meal. Sansho, or mountain, pepper is the Japanese cousin of Szechuan peppercorns, but more subtle. Neither is a peppercorn at all, but the seed pod of the prickly ash tree and, as well as the pods, the young shoots, flowers and bitter berries are also used in cooking. Shichimi togarashi, the Japanese seven-spice blend, has sansho as one of its constituents. The Japanese ingredients in this soup are quite widely available and they can be used in other recipes, so keep a stock in your pantry. The soup is definitely worth making – serve it as the Japanese do, in beautiful lacquer bowls.

To make the dashi, put the kombu in a large saucepan and add 550 ml water. Bring to the boil and immediately remove the kombu (don't let it boil or it will become bitter).

Add the bonito flakes to the boiling water, simmer gently for 2–3 minutes, then remove from the heat. Let stand for a few minutes until the bonito settles to the bottom of the pan. Strain through a sieve lined with muslin and reserve the liquid. Alternatively, add 1–2 teaspoons instant dashi powder to the boiling water and stir to dissolve.

Meanwhile, soak the wakame in a large bowl of water for 10–15 minutes until fully opened. Drain and cut into small pieces.

Put the miso paste into a cup or bowl and mix with a few spoonfuls of dashi. Return the dashi to a low heat and add the diluted miso paste. Add the wakame and tofu to the pan and turn up the heat. Just before it reaches boiling point, add the spring onion and immediately remove from the heat. Do not boil.

Serve hot in individual soup bowls with a little shichimi togarashi for sprinkling.

***Note** Instant dashi powder is widely available in larger supermarkets and Japanese stores. Labelled 'dashi-no-moto', it is freeze-dried and very convenient. Use 1–2 teaspoons for this recipe.

- Thai basil
- coriander

indonesian beef and coconut soup

750 g trimmed braising beef, cut into small chunks

7 white peppercorns

3 cm fresh galangal or ginger, peeled and sliced

1 teaspoon freshly grated nutmeg

¼ teaspoon ground turmeric

325 ml coconut milk

sea salt

spice paste

2–3 tablespoons groundnut oil

1 teaspoon ground coriander

7 white peppercorns

4 red bird's eye chillies

2 teaspoons brown sugar

1 garlic clove, chopped

5 fresh Thai basil (or sweet basil) leaves

a large handful of fresh coriander, about 25 g, coarsely chopped, plus extra leaves to garnish (optional)

8 pink Thai shallots or 1 regular shallot

a few cardamom seeds (not pods)

2 cm fresh ginger, peeled and chopped

a small piece of toasted shrimp paste* or 1 teaspoon anchovy paste mixed with 1 tablespoon fish sauce

serves 4–6

This strongly spiced and flavoured soup has slices of meat swimming in plenty of creamy broth. It is quintessentially Indonesian in its spicing, influenced by the nation's diverse population and topography. Wave after wave of settlers entered Indonesia long ago, from Malays, Indians and Chinese to Arab traders. Living on the world's largest archipelago and comprising around 350 ethnic groups, Indonesians are a varied people and so is their cuisine. What comes across in dishes like this soup is a fascinating mixture of spices and flavours.

Put all the spice paste ingredients in a food processor or blender and blend to a thick paste, adding a dash of water to keep the blades turning if necessary. Set aside.

Put the beef, peppercorns, galangal, nutmeg, turmeric and salt into a saucepan, add 1.5 litres water and bring to the boil, skimming off the foam as it rises to the surface. Stir, reduce the heat and simmer uncovered for about 1½ hours, until the meat is mostly tender and the stock is well reduced.

Strain the beef, discarding the galangal slices and peppercorns, but reserving the beef and stock. Return the stock to the pan, then stir in the spice paste. Bring to the boil, then reduce the heat, add the beef and simmer for 5 minutes, stirring regularly.

Finally, add the coconut milk and simmer gently for a few minutes. Serve the soup on its own or with a small mound of plain rice for each person. Garnish with coriander, if liked. You could also serve it with an Indonesian spiced rice like nasi goreng, but the soup should then be eaten separately.

***Note** Dried shrimp paste is also known as trassi, beluchan or blachan. Extremely pungent, it gives a distinctive taste to South-east Asian food and is worth hunting down in a Thai, Malay or Indonesian food store. Use a very small piece (about ½ teaspoon) and always toast it before using. To toast, simply wrap a piece in aluminium foil and toast it in a hot oven until it darkens – a few minutes per side. It's a good idea to open the windows in your kitchen when using shrimp paste as it leaves a pervasive scent!

- cayenne pepper
- sumac
- flat leaf parsley
- mint (left)

mint and parsley salad

turkish ksir

85 g bulghur wheat

2 tomatoes, halved, cored and chopped, with the juices reserved

1 red onion or shallot, finely chopped and soaked in a little lemon juice

½ cucumber, peeled in strips, deseeded and cut into cubes

2 tablespoons extra virgin olive oil

a pinch of cayenne pepper

1 teaspoon ground sumac*

a bunch of flat leaf parsley, plus extra to garnish (optional)

a bunch of mint

sea salt and freshly ground black pepper

lemon and lime wedges, to serve

serves 2–4

This Turkish salad of bulghur wheat and herbs is similar to the more familiar Lebanese tabbouleh. Chopping the mint just before you are ready to serve the salad prevents it turning black. Traditionally, this salad is served with pickled vegetables on boiled vine leaves, but it also works well served simply with lemon and lime wedges.

Put the bulghur in a bowl and cover with 150 ml cold water. Let stand for about 40 minutes to absorb the liquid.

Put the bulghur in a sieve and squeeze out any excess water. Transfer to a serving bowl, then add the tomatoes and their juices, onion, cucumber, olive oil, cayenne, salt and pepper and half the sumac.

Remove the leaves from the parsley and mint and chop them coarsely. Add to the salad, toss gently and sprinkle with the remaining sumac. Garnish with parsley, if liked, and serve with lemon and lime wedges.

***Note** The reddish-purple sumac berry is a spice tasting a little of lemons. It was used by the Romans before lemons, to do the same job. It is sold ground finely and is available from Middle Eastern stores and spice shops. It's a lovely addition to this salad. If you can't find it, add the freshly squeezed juice of ½ lemon.

• savory

savory feta salad
with sugar snap peas, edamame and watermelon

200 g edamame (fresh soy beans)
200 g broad beans, shelled
150 g sugar snap peas
½ small watermelon
4 tablespoons sunflower oil
200 g feta cheese
young leaves from 5 sprigs of savory
freshly ground black pepper

serves 6

Winter and summer savory are two different plants: summer savory is an annual with tender leaves and softer stalk, while the winter version is an evergreen perennial and is a little stronger and more resinous in flavour. Both are good with beans, including edamame (fresh soy beans). Although the leaves of both summer and winter savory will toughen over the summer, they still retain a wonderful flavour. The spicy, peppery taste is at its best in early summer, ready for the first crop of beans. When cut back savagely after flowering, a new crop of tender leaves will appear before autumn.

Bring a large saucepan of unsalted water to the boil. Add the edamame and broad beans and blanch for 2 minutes. Drain and refresh in cold water, then remove the edamame from their pods and the broad beans from their skins. Put into a large serving bowl.

Blanch the sugar snaps in boiling salted water for 30 seconds, drain, refresh under cold running water, drain again, then slice lengthways. Add to the serving bowl with the edamame and broad beans.

Peel and slice the watermelon over a bowl to catch the juices. Cut the watermelon into small wedges, as shown, then add to the salad. Squeeze a few pieces to get about 3 tablespoons of juice in a separate bowl. Whisk the oil into the watermelon juice, then pour over the salad.

Crumble the feta over the top, sprinkle with young savory leaves and black pepper, then serve.

tomato and lentil salad

adis ma bandoora

200 g brown lentils
5 tablespoons extra virgin olive oil
1 onion, halved and thinly sliced
400 g cherry tomatoes, quartered
2 teaspoons sumac, plus extra to serve*
sea salt and freshly ground black pepper

serves 4–6

This salad is from Lebanon and Syria, but similar lentil dishes can be found all round the eastern Mediterranean, from Egypt to Turkey. Although not Middle Eastern, Umbrian (Italian brown) lentils work well in this dish as they hold their texture and are particularly flavoursome. Sumac is a popular Middle Eastern spice, enjoyed for its sour flavour. Other popular spices in the Levant include allspice and caraway.

Put the lentils into a bowl, cover with plenty of cold water and soak for 2 hours or according to the instructions on the packet. Drain, transfer to a saucepan, add a pinch of salt and cover with boiling water. Return to the boil, then reduce the heat and simmer for 15 minutes or until *al dente* (tender but still firm). Drain well and set aside.

Clean the pan, add 2 tablespoons of the olive oil and heat well. Add the onion and fry gently for about 8 minutes until softened and translucent. Remove from the heat and add the lentils, tomatoes, sumac, salt, pepper and the remaining oil. Stir gently with a wooden spoon and serve as a side dish, with extra sumac served separately.

***Note** If you can't find sumac but would like to try this salad, opt for a completely different, but still Middle Eastern, flavour. In the Levant, caraway is used in many ways, and will give this salad a light anise flavour rather than the sour edge provided by the sumac. Add 1 teaspoon caraway seeds when you heat the oil, then proceed with the recipe.

- lemongrass
- kaffir lime leaves
- mint
- Thai sweet basil

thai spicy squid salad

yam pla muek

This spicy Thai squid salad makes a delicious summer starter, full of light and interesting flavours – all you need to titillate the palate for the dishes to follow. If Thai mint is available, do use it. Though its fragrant leaves look a little ragged, they taste simply fabulous when chopped, adding a hotness that's certainly not to be missed. Thai mint and basil are available in bunches in Asian and South-east Asian markets, and plants are sold in some specialist herb nurseries for you to grow in your garden. Remember that they come from a hot climate, so keep them out of the frost.

750 g fresh squid tubes, with tentacles

100 g pink Thai shallots

1 stalk of lemongrass, trimmed and thinly sliced

2 long red chillies, deseeded and thinly sliced

3 kaffir lime leaves, rolled up and thinly sliced

2 cm fresh ginger, peeled, thinly sliced, then cut into thin matchsticks

3 spring onions, sliced diagonally

dressing

2 garlic cloves, crushed

2 medium red chillies, finely chopped

freshly squeezed juice of 4 small limes

4 tablespoons Thai fish sauce

to serve

2 tablespoons chopped mint or Thai mint

a handful of Thai sweet basil leaves

serves 6

To make the dressing, pound the garlic and chillies using a mortar and pestle, then add the lime juice and fish sauce. Transfer to a serving bowl and chill in the refrigerator until required.

Cut the squid tubes down one edge to make 1 large piece. Score the inside with a diamond pattern and cut each piece diagonally in half.

Prepare a saucepan of boiling salted water and drop the squid into the water in 2 batches. As soon as the squid pieces curl up, leave for another minute, then drain immediately. Make sure you bring the water back to the boil again before dropping in the next batch. Add the squid to the chilled dressing in the serving bowl while still hot.

Add the shallots, lemongrass, chillies, kaffir lime leaves, ginger and spring onions to the bowl and toss gently. Serve sprinkled with chopped mint and whole Thai sweet basil leaves.

- garlic
- ginger
- chilli (left)

bulgogi

Bulgogi is a Korean delight – as popular with tourists as it is with the locals. In restaurants the beef strips are grilled on table-top grills, but you could also cook them on foil over hot coals or sear them in a very hot pan – a method that's commonplace in the home. Ginger and toasted sesame oil are included in the marinade, while chillies make their inevitable appearance, though the amount is up to you. Bulgogi is a starter that can be made and served in two ways. Always sliced very thinly, the beef strips can be wide or narrow. The wide ones are served with rice and condiments, while the narrow ones are rolled up in lettuce leaves, which is an entirely satisfying way of eating this dish.

marinade

1 large sirloin steak, 3–4 cm thick, about 500 g, trimmed of fat

2 tablespoons tamari or other soy sauce

1 teaspoon toasted sesame oil

1–2 teaspoons sugar

1 garlic clove, crushed

3 cm fresh ginger, peeled and finely grated

2 spring onions, trimmed and chopped

1–2 bird's eye chillies, red or green, deseeded and chopped

a pinch of sea salt

lettuce leaves, to serve

kimchi

1 teaspoon sugar

2 tablespoons rice vinegar

1 large garlic clove, crushed

a pinch of sea salt

250 g daikon (mooli or white radish), peeled and grated

a ridged stove-top grill pan (optional)

serves 4

Make the kimchi 1–3 days before using. Put the sugar, vinegar, garlic and salt into a bowl. Put the grated radish into a cloth and squeeze well to remove excess water. Add the radish to the bowl and mix until well coated. While the jar is still hot, pour the kimchi into the jar and seal tightly. Let cool, then refrigerate until ready to use.

Freeze the steak for 1 hour so it will be easy to slice. Remove the steak from the freezer, then slice very thinly crossways.

To make the marinade, put the tamari, sesame oil and sugar into a bowl and whisk well. Stir in the garlic, ginger, spring onions, chillies and salt. Add the beef strips, mix well to coat, then cover and refrigerate for several hours to develop the flavours.

Heat a lightly greased ridged stove-top grill pan or frying pan until very hot. Sear the strips of steak briefly on both sides until just done, working in batches so you don't overcrowd the pan. Either pile onto a large serving plate or divide between 4 plates and serve with lettuce and kimchi.

- tamarind
- Szechuan pepper
- Thai basil

vegetarian cashew salad
with tamarind dressing

8 Chinese leaves (Chinese or Napa cabbage)

1 large carrot

1 cucumber, about 20 cm long, halved, deseeded, cut into 5-cm sections, then thinly sliced lengthways

6 spring onions, sliced diagonally

8 slices dried mango, chopped

75 g cashews, toasted in a dry frying pan, then coarsely crushed

tamarind dressing*

50 g lump tamarind (an apricot-sized piece), or about 2 teaspoons tamarind paste, to taste

½ teaspoon Szechuan peppercorns, lightly toasted in a dry frying pan, then coarsely crushed

2 teaspoons sesame oil

1 garlic clove, finely chopped

½ teaspoon golden caster sugar or jaggery (palm sugar), to taste

about 2 tablespoons chopped Thai basil, regular coriander or Vietnamese coriander

sea salt

serves 4

**You can substitute the similar but thicker Vietnamese Tamarind Dip (page 179) for this dressing.*

This is a simple vegetarian salad with fragrant South-east Asian flavours (Vietnamese and Thai), but also with a hint of Chinese. It is versatile too, because other ingredients can be added according to the season or the tastes of your guests. Sour tamarind and Szechuan pepper form an unusual partnership in the dressing – a combination of sour and hot. Tamarind is available in lump form, or as a ready-made paste. Although the latter is very handy, making your own paste is easy and the freshness is hard to beat. If you prefer, you can use the Vietnamese Tamarind Dip (page 179) instead of the dressing.

To make the tamarind water for the dressing, put the tamarind into a small glass bowl. Add 250 ml warm water and let soak for 15 minutes. Then squeeze the tamarind through your fingers in the water and continue until all of it has been squeezed into a pulp. Press through a sieve.

Put 6 tablespoons of the strained tamarind water, the Szechuan pepper, sesame oil, garlic, sugar and Thai basil into a screw-top jar and shake well. Set aside. (Any remaining tamarind water can be boiled in a pan, cooled, then refrigerated for later use.)

Stack the Chinese leaves on top of each other and slice them finely. Grate the carrot into long sticks using the large blade of a box grater, or slice finely into long strips. Divide the shredded leaves between 4 plates, add a layer of grated carrot, then the cucumber strips. Top with the spring onions and dried mango. Sprinkle the dressing over the salad, top with the cashews, then serve.

Variations Instead of Chinese leaves, you can use another crisp lettuce, such as Little Gem. Alternatively, omit the leaves and make a simple carrot and spring onion salad. For a non-vegetarian version of this dish, add 2 poached skinless chicken breasts, cooled and pulled into shreds, or 2 duck breasts, cooked in a stove-top grill pan, then sliced.

starters & light meals

- epazote (left)
- coriander
- oregano
- chilli

grilled chilli herb polenta
with papaya mojo

Epazote is a Mexican herb available dried, and occasionally fresh, in Latino markets. The word derives from its ancient Aztec name. It grows like a weed in the garden and has a very distinctive odour – a bit like bleach. It is famous as a partner for beans, because it counteracts their gaseous tendencies.

a small bunch of coriander
4 sprigs of oregano
a handful of chives
250 g quick-cook polenta
50 g unsalted butter, cut into pieces
50 g Asiago vecchio cheese, grated
2 long red chillies, deseeded and finely chopped
sea salt and freshly ground black pepper
olive oil spray

papaya mojo

75 g shallots, thinly sliced
grated zest and freshly squeezed juice of 1 unwaxed lime
5 tablespoons olive oil
1 large papaya, peeled and cut into cubes
a small bunch of coriander
a handful of chives, chopped
sea salt and freshly ground black pepper

epazote beans

100 g black beans, rinsed and drained
2 sprigs of fresh epazote or a pinch of dried

a baking sheet or dish, 23 x 32 cm, oiled

a ridged stove-top grill pan

serves 6

To prepare the epazote beans, put them in a bowl, cover with cold water and let soak overnight. Drain, rinse and put them in a saucepan. Cover again with cold water and bring to the boil for 5 minutes. Lower the heat, add the epazote and simmer until just cooked – about 1 hour.

Remove the leaves from the coriander and oregano stalks and chop them coarsely with the chives. Bring 1 litre water to the boil and add a pinch of salt. Add the polenta all at once, whisking constantly. As it thickens, stir in the butter and cheese. Mix well, then fold in the herbs, chillies, salt and pepper.

Pour into the prepared baking sheet, smooth the top with a damp palette knife and let cool. Leave uncovered and chill until 30 minutes before finishing.

To make the papaya mojo, put the shallots and lime juice in a bowl, stir gently, then gradually stir in the olive oil, papaya, salt and pepper. Remove the coriander leaves from the stalks and chop coarsely, then add to the mojo with the chives. Fold the mojo into the bean mixture.

Carefully take the polenta out of the baking sheet and transfer to a board. Cut into 12 wedges. Heat a ridged stove-top grill pan and, when it starts to smoke, lower the heat a little, spray with olive oil and add the polenta. Grill on the top side for 2 minutes, then turn the pieces 180 degrees to create a criss-cross pattern. Cook for 1 minute more. Serve hot with the mojo and beans and garnished with coriander, if liked.

- chives
- chervil
- tarragon (left)

baked ricotta

and herb terrine

250 g fresh ricotta cheese

4 eggs

1 egg yolk

20 g plain flour

50 g pecorino cheese, grated*

½ teaspoon coarsely crushed dried green peppercorns

a small bunch of chives, with flowers if possible

a small bunch of chervil

a small bunch of tarragon

to serve

3 tomatoes, preferably an heirloom variety such as Green Zebra

herb oil (page 170)

a 500 g loaf tin, greased with butter

a roasting tin or similar dish, to hold the loaf tin

serves 6

If chives are in flower, pluck the petals apart and sprinkle them over each serving. Full-flavoured heirloom tomatoes (sold in specialist greengrocers and farmers' markets) drizzled with homemade herb oil make a delicious accompaniment for this dish.

Put the ricotta in a bowl and beat with a wooden spoon until smooth. Beat in the eggs and the extra egg yolk, one at a time. Put the flour, pecorino and pepper in a separate bowl, stir well, then beat into the ricotta mixture.

Reserve a few chives, then coarsely chop the remaining chives with the chervil and tarragon. Fold them into the ricotta. Spoon the mixture into the prepared loaf tin, stand it in the roasting tin and fill with enough water to come halfway up the outside of the loaf tin. (This is called a bain-marie or water bath.) Bake, uncovered, in a preheated oven at 180°C (350°F) Gas 4 for 35–45 minutes until risen, golden and set.

Remove the loaf tin from the roasting tin (as the terrine cools it will shrink away from the sides). After about 8 minutes, run a knife around the sides of the terrine, then carefully invert it onto a serving dish or board and cut into slices. Cut the tomatoes into wedges. Sprinkle the terrine and tomatoes with the herb oil, add the reserved whole chives and chive flowers, if available, and serve. If serving cold, let cool for at least 15 minutes.

***Note** Pecorino is a sheep's milk cheese, stronger than Parmesan (which could be used instead).

- curry leaves
- chilli
- coriander
- mint

mint and coriander salsa
with singaras

500 g potatoes suitable for mashing, cut into chips

8 curry leaves or 3 bay leaves

1 tablespoon vegetable oil, plus extra for deep-frying

2 onions, finely chopped

2 garlic cloves, crushed

2 medium-hot green chillies, deseeded and finely chopped

1 teaspoon ground cumin

a small bunch of coriander, leaves chopped

16 small spring roll wrappers (13 cm square), cut in 2, or 8 large (25 cm square), cut in 3

sea salt

mint and coriander salsa

5 pink Thai shallots or 2 regular shallots, finely chopped

finely grated zest and juice of 1 unwaxed lime

½ teaspoon sugar (optional)

2 ripe mangoes, peeled and cut into small cubes

2 red chillies, deseeded and finely chopped

a small bunch of mint, finely chopped

a small bunch of coriander, finely chopped

an electric deep-fryer (optional)

serves 6–8

Singaras are a kind of Indian samosa, but you can make them (large or small) with spring roll wrappers rather than heavier pastry. They are wonderful on their own, with a squeeze of lemon or with a salsa like this one. Another idea is to serve them with bowls of coriander, mint leaves and finely sliced red onion, so people can take a little of each with a bite of singara – the result is a terrific snack to serve with drinks. The singaras can be made in advance, then reheated or served cold.

Put the freshly cut potato chips in a saucepan of cold water, add the curry leaves, bring to the boil, then add salt. When the potatoes are soft, drain and cover with a clean tea towel for 5 minutes, then remove the curry leaves and chop into the potatoes. If using bay leaves instead of curry leaves, discard them. Put the potatoes in a bowl.

Heat the oil in a frying pan, add the onions and garlic and fry until soft and very pale golden. Mash the potatoes, then stir in the onions, garlic, chillies, cumin and coriander. Stir briefly and let cool.

Put a strip of spring roll wrapper on a work surface and put a teaspoon of mixture in the bottom left hand corner. Fold over to the right to make a triangle. Continue folding, end to end, then wet the edge with a little water and press to seal.

Fill a wok or deep-fryer one-third full with oil, or to the manufacturer's recommended level, and heat to 200°C (400°F). Add the singaras in batches of 2–3 and fry for about 2 minutes each, turning occasionally. Remove and drain on kitchen paper while you cook the remainder.

To make the mint and coriander salsa, put the shallots in a bowl, add the lime zest and juice, and sugar, if using, and set aside for 5 minutes. Just before serving, stir in the mangoes, chillies, mint and coriander. Serve with the singaras.

basil mayonnaise
with crispy prawns

120 g rice stick noodles, broken into 3

24 medium uncooked prawns, shelled, deveined and tail shells intact

2 sheets of nori seaweed, cut into 24 strips

sunflower oil, for deep-frying

basil mayonnaise

leaves from a large bunch of basil, about 75 g

1 egg yolk

¼ teaspoon salt

1 tablespoon cider vinegar

75 ml olive oil

75 ml sunflower oil

freshly squeezed juice of 1 lime

an electric deep-fryer (optional)

serves 4–6

There is life beyond basil and tomatoes. Basil is wonderful with seafood, and great with mayonnaise. Though spectacular, this dish is not fiddly to make because you can be quite haphazard about it. The noodles frizz up when fried, so all imperfections disappear.

To make the basil mayonnaise, bring a saucepan of water to the boil, add all the basil and wilt briefly. Drain and run under cold water to cool quickly. Squeeze out as much water as possible and pat the basil dry with kitchen paper.

Put the basil in a food processor or blender with the egg yolk, salt, vinegar and 1 tablespoon of oil. Blend to a purée and, with the motor running, gradually pour in the rest of the oils to achieve a thick consistency. Spoon into a bowl and add the lime juice to taste.

Fill a wok or deep-fryer one-third full with sunflower oil, or to the manufacturer's recommended level, and heat to 200°C (400°F), or until a piece of noodle puffs up immediately. Bind the lengths of noodle onto the prawns using a strip of the seaweed – dampen the ends of the seaweed and seal together. Add to the hot oil in batches and fry until the noodles puff up and turn slightly golden, about 1 minute. Drain on kitchen paper and trim the ends of the prawns neatly. Serve with the basil mayonnaise as a dip.

Note You can use the basil mayonnaise with other things, such as big, homemade chips with masses of fried basil leaves.

dill-marinated salmon
with pancakes and sabayon

1 kg salmon fillet
2 tablespoons gin
a large bunch of dill
5 tablespoons sea salt flakes
3 tablespoons caster sugar

pancakes

125 g self-raising flour
a pinch of salt
¼ teaspoon baking powder
1 egg
1 teaspoon Dijon mustard
180 ml milk
1 tablespoon freshly chopped dill leaves
sunflower oil, for cooking

sabayon

2 egg yolks
1 tablespoon thin honey
2 tablespoons Dijon mustard
3 tablespoons gin

a poffertjes pan, aebleskiver pan, blini pan or crêpe pan

serves 6–8: makes about 36 pancakes

This traditionally-cured salmon takes 36–48 hours to cure and the flavour of the dill penetrates right into the fish. A whole fillet of salmon is great to serve at a party, but if you want it for a smaller group, just halve the recipe. To make the pancakes, a special Dutch pan, called a poffertjes pan, is ideal – it has 19 indentations so the little pancakes can be cooked in large batches. Instead, you can use a doughnut pan, such as an aebleskiver or blini pan, or make tiny ones, a few at a time, in a regular crêpe pan. A flavoured sabayon is served instead of the usual dill and mustard sauce.

Put the salmon on a board flesh side up and rub with the gin. Remove the dill fronds from the thick stalks, chop them, then mix with the salt and sugar and rub into the flesh. Put in a non-metallic dish and cover with clingfilm. Put a board on top with weights on top of that (2 heavy food cans are suitable). Chill for 36–48 hours. Slice thinly at a 45-degree angle to serve.

To make the pancake batter, sift the flour, salt and baking powder into a bowl. Make a hollow in the middle, add the egg, mustard and half the milk. Whisk gently, then slowly add the rest of the milk to make a smooth batter. Add the chopped dill and whisk into the mixture.

Lightly oil the chosen pan. Heat the pan and fill each indentation with batter almost to the top. Fry them until their undersides are brown, then flip them and cook the other side. Keep warm while the remaining batter is cooked.

Just before serving, make the sabayon sauce. Put the egg yolks, honey, mustard and gin in a bowl set over a saucepan of barely simmering water so the bowl doesn't touch the water. Using a hand-held electric beater, whisk until the volume has increased and the mixture is foaming and holding its shape. Top each pancake with a slice of salmon and a spoonful of sabayon and garnish with dill.

- chilli
- ginger
- garlic
- star anise (left)
- black pepper

vietnamese spiced squid

Vietnamese cuisine is notable for its use of herbs, while spices, when used, are balanced and often gentle. However, southern Vietnamese cooking uses spices such as ginger, galangal, star anise, tamarind, chillies and occasionally turmeric, five-spice powder and curry powder. This appetizing starter of stuffed baby squid, spiced with star anise, ginger and pepper is a typical example. Nuóc cham is the traditional Vietnamese dipping sauce, but you could use soy sauce or chilli sauce.

25 g cellophane rice noodles (rice vermicelli), about 1 small bundle

90 ml groundnut oil

3 spring onions, chopped

3 cm fresh ginger, peeled and grated

2 garlic cloves, chopped

16 prepared, cleaned baby squid with tentacles reserved*

325 g pork mince

2–3 'petals' of 1 star anise, finely crushed (about ¼ teaspoon ground)

¼ teaspoon cracked black pepper

1 tablespoon Thai or Vietnamese fish sauce

a pinch of sugar

a pinch of sea salt

a handful of mixed Asian herbs, to serve

nuóc cham dipping sauce

1 garlic clove, crushed

1 red bird's eye chilli, thinly sliced

2 tablespoons sugar

freshly squeezed juice of ½ lime

4 tablespoons Thai or Vietnamese fish sauce

cocktail sticks

makes 16

To make the dipping sauce, use a mortar and pestle to grind the garlic, chilli and sugar to form a paste. Stir in the lime juice, fish sauce and about 3 tablespoons water. Transfer to a dipping bowl.

To prepare the stuffing, put the noodles in a bowl, pour over boiling water and let soak for 4 minutes or according to the instructions on the packet. Drain well, coarsely chop the noodles and transfer to a large bowl.

Put 1 tablespoon of the groundnut oil into a wok, heat well, swirl to coat, then add the spring onions, ginger and garlic. Stir-fry for a few minutes until softened, then add to the bowl. Chop the squid tentacles and add to the ingredients in the bowl. Add the pork mince, star anise, black pepper, fish sauce, sugar and salt and mix well. Stuff the squid bodies with the pork mixture, leaving a little space at the top, and secure closed with cocktail sticks.

Heat the remaining oil in a frying pan and add the squid. Cook gently for 10–12 minutes, until lightly browned in places and cooked through. Slice the squid or leave them whole, then serve with fresh herbs and nuóc cham.

***Note** To prepare the squid, cut off the tentacles and chop them coarsely. Cut off and discard the eye sections. Rinse out the bodies, discarding the tiny transparent quill. If you can't find squid with tentacles, buy an extra body, chop it coarsely, then add to the stuffing mixture.

- coriander
- lemongrass
- chilli

stir-fried peanut prawns
with coriander noodles

Similar to the popular dish, Pad Thai, this recipe is dryer, less sweet and omits certain key ingredients such as eggs, substituting stir-fry vegetables instead. Tiny, blindingly hot bird's eye chillies are an essential spice in South-east Asian cuisine: if you would prefer this dish less hot, use another kind of chilli or reduce the number.

150 g rice stick noodles
5 tablespoons groundnut oil
a pinch of ground coriander
2 kaffir lime leaves, 1 thinly sliced or crushed and 1 left whole
1 stalk of lemongrass, outer leaves discarded, the remainder very finely chopped
3–4 red bird's eye chillies, deseeded and thinly sliced
3 spring onions, chopped
1 large garlic clove, crushed
100 g vegetables such as broccoli, cauliflower, red pepper, asparagus tips, onion, sugar snap peas and string beans, all cut into bite-sized pieces
a pinch of sugar
3 tablespoons Thai fish sauce
250 g uncooked, shelled tiger prawns, deveined (about 400 g, shell-on)
freshly squeezed juice of 1 lemon
150 g dry-roasted peanuts, coarsely ground
25 g fresh coriander, finely chopped

to serve

a handful of coriander leaves, chopped
a few green bird's eye chillies, deseeded and thinly sliced
2 spring onions, green part only, thinly sliced
a handful of beansprouts

serves 4

Put the noodles into a bowl and cover with boiling water. Let soak for 4 minutes or according to the instructions on the packet. Drain, return to the bowl and cover with cold water until ready to serve. Bring a kettle of water to the boil and have it ready to reheat.

Put 3 tablespoons of the groundnut oil into a non-stick wok, heat well and swirl to coat. Add the ground coriander, kaffir lime leaves, lemongrass, red chillies and spring onions and stir-fry briefly. Add the garlic and stir-fry again for 20 seconds. Add the prepared vegetables, sugar and 2 tablespoons of the fish sauce and stir-fry over medium-high heat for 1 minute.

Add the prawns and lemon juice and stir-fry for 1 minute, then add half the ground peanuts. Mix well, add the remaining tablespoon of fish sauce and cook for 2 more minutes or until the prawns turn pink.

Meanwhile, drain the noodles again and return them to the bowl. Cover with boiling water, drain and return to the bowl. Add the remaining groundnut oil, toss to coat, add the fresh coriander and toss again. Add the noodles to the wok, toss to coat, then serve immediately topped with coriander leaves, green chillies, spring onions, beansprouts and the remaining peanuts.

- thyme
- marjoram
- sweet cicely (left)

chicken liver mousse

150 g unsalted butter
1 garlic clove, crushed
leaves from 5 sprigs of thyme or lemon thyme
500 g chicken livers, trimmed
75 ml dry Marsala wine
leaves from 3 sprigs of marjoram
sea salt and freshly ground black pepper

to serve

sweet cicely leaves and flowers, or chervil
thinly sliced walnut bread

1 bowl or 6 small ramekins

serves 6

This variation of the classic chicken liver pâte uses the Italian Marsala instead of French brandy. The top of the pâté can be decorated with sweet cicely leaves and flowers. If these aren't available, use chervil or fine flat leaf parsley leaves with a few pink peppercorns instead. This is great to take on a picnic, or to serve as a starter for a dinner party – it tastes delicious served with toasted wafer-thin slices of walnut bread.

Heat a frying pan over medium heat and add about 15 g of the butter, the garlic, half the thyme and half the chicken livers. Cook the livers for about 1½ minutes on each side (they should still be slightly pink inside), then transfer to a food processor. Add another 15 g butter to the frying pan and cook the remaining livers and thyme in the same way. Deglaze the pan with the Marsala, then add to the food processor. Add the marjoram, 45 g of the remaining butter and a little salt and pepper.

Blend until smooth, then transfer to a sieve set over a bowl and push the mixture through the sieve with the back of a ladle.

Spoon the resulting mousse into the serving bowl or ramekins and tap on the work surface to settle the mixture. Melt the remaining butter in a small saucepan and pour over the mousse, leaving the sediment in the bottom of the pan. Arrange the sweet cicely and flowers on top and chill until needed. The mousse will keep for several days in the refrigerator. Serve with thinly sliced walnut bread.

- black pepper
- flat leaf parsley (left)
- bay leaves
- thyme

parsleyed ham

jambon persillé

1 kg best-quality cured pork or ham steak (gammon), soaked overnight

1 medium veal knuckle, chopped into pieces

1 shallot

2 carrots

¼ teaspoon black peppercorns

a large bunch of flat leaf parsley

2 bay leaves

a large sprig of thyme

4 sheets of leaf gelatine or 2½ tablespoons powdered gelatine (optional)

150 ml white wine

1 tablespoon tarragon vinegar

3 egg whites and shells

to serve

crusty bread

radishes

gherkins

serves 6–8

This Burgundian Easter classic requires lots of very fresh flat leaf parsley and a beautiful piece of cured ham, plus some jelly-making ingredients and a large pinch of commitment!

Put the pork or ham, veal, shallot, carrots and peppercorns in a large saucepan. Strip the leaves off the parsley and put them in a plastic bag in the refrigerator. Tie up the parsley stalks, bay leaves and thyme with string to make a bouquet garni and add to the pan. Cover with water and heat to a gentle simmer with the water hardly moving. Cook for about 1½ hours or until very tender.

Lift the meat out onto a plate and let cool. Cover and put in the refrigerator. Simmer the liquid for another 30 minutes. Lift out the knuckle and strain the liquid through a sieve into a bowl and let cool. When cool, measure 750 ml and put in the refrigerator overnight (the remaining liquid can be used for soup).

If the liquid has set to a firm jelly, there will be no need to use the gelatine (otherwise soak and use the gelatine after clarifying the liquid). Simply skim off any fat and spoon the jelly into a saucepan. If it has not set, use a baster to extract liquid from the centre and transfer to a saucepan, leaving the fat behind. Heat until just melted, then add the wine and vinegar.

Put the egg whites and shells in a bowl and whisk well. Add to the pan and, whisking constantly, gradually bring to the boil. As soon as the froth rises to the top of the pan, stop whisking and remove from the heat. Let settle for 4 minutes.

Take care that the crust on top does not break, then heat the liquid once again just to the boil. As soon as it rises, take off the heat and leave for 10 minutes.

Meanwhile cut the ham into small pieces and discard any fat. Gently strain the liquid through a sieve set over a bowl lined with a double thickness of muslin. Cool until it has almost set to jelly. Chop the reserved parsley and add to the jelly with the ham. Spoon into a glass bowl (or several small bowls) right to the top, then let set in the refrigerator. Serve with crusty bread, radishes and gherkins.

- Thai green curry paste
- Thai basil

thai green chicken curry

800 ml canned coconut milk

1 recipe Thai Green Curry Paste (page 179) or 7 tablespoons ready-made paste

4 boneless skinless chicken breasts, preferably free-range or organic, thickly sliced

2 tablespoons Thai fish sauce

¼ teaspoon brown sugar or palm sugar

to serve

Thai basil leaves or chopped coriander

1 lime, cut into 4 wedges

3 bird's eye chillies, halved lengthways (optional)

serves 4

This famous Thai curry is full of the fragrance of fresh spices and herbs for which Thai cuisine is renowned. Coconut milk tempers the heat of the tiny bird's eye chillies in the green curry paste (although this is a mild version) and adds the essential creaminess. Throughout South-east Asia, although dried spices are certainly used, the fresh versions are more typical. The spice trade grew out of the desire, especially in Europe, for the flavours of Asian spices. These were mostly used fresh in their own countries, but they could only be exported in their dry form. Modern modes of transport and polytunnel agriculture mean that fresh chillies, ginger and similar spices are now available in supermarkets around the world.

Put a ladle of the coconut milk into a wok or deep frying pan, add the curry paste and stir-fry to release the aromas. Add the chicken and stir-fry to coat with the spices. Add the remaining coconut milk, bring to the boil, reduce the heat and gently simmer for about 8 minutes, or until the chicken is cooked through and still tender.

Add the fish sauce and sugar and cook for a further 1 minute. Transfer to a serving bowl, sprinkle with the Thai basil and add the lime wedges and chillies, if liked. Serve with other Thai dishes and fragrant Thai rice.

Note Thais usually serve all dishes at once. Steamed rice is the basis of the meal, and diners take a share of each dish to eat with rice. One dish is eaten at a time – never several at once. A fork and spoon is used, with the fork being used to push the food onto the spoon.

- zahtar spice mix
- baharat spice mix

lamb kebab mashwi

with spiced flatbreads

In the Arabian Gulf States, where many kinds of kebabs are popular, kebab mashwi is one of the most delicious. This recipe uses several regional herbs and spices. From India to North Africa, kebabs are usually served with flatbreads. In these areas, people eat with their fingers, so the bread is used to pull the kebabs off the skewers.

750 g trimmed, boneless leg of lamb, twice minced (ask the butcher to put the meat through the mincer twice)

1 large onion, finely chopped

1 teaspoon sea salt

4 tablespoons chopped fresh marjoram

2 tablespoons chopped fresh mint

2 teaspoons Baharat (page 174)

1 teaspoon loomi (dried lime) powder (optional)*

mafrouda (spiced flatbreads)**

450 g white bread flour

1 sachet (1 tablespoon) easy-blend dried yeast

1 teaspoon sea salt

¼ teaspoon sugar

1 tablespoon extra virgin olive oil

2 teaspoons Zahtar (page 174)

to serve

2 shallots, sliced and soaked in lemon juice

1 tablespoon chopped mint

Greek yoghurt mixed with a little tahini paste

sumac, to sprinkle (optional)

metal skewers

serves 4

***see note on dough and batter, page 4*

To make the flatbreads, put the flour in a large bowl, make a well in the centre and add the yeast. Gradually add enough tepid water to make a pliable dough, about 250 ml. Start bringing the flour into the centre. Add the salt, sugar and olive oil and knead well for 5 minutes. Add the zahtar and continue kneading for 5 minutes. Although this is leavened bread, the dough should not rest. Form into 4 balls and roll out into long rectangular shapes or rounds.

Prick the flatbreads all over with a fork. Arrange on baking sheets and bake in a preheated fan oven at 220°C (425°F) Gas 7 for about 2 minutes, then turn and cook for a further 2 minutes. (If using a regular oven, adjust the cooking time and temperature according to the manufacturer's instructions.) Wrap the flatbreads in aluminium foil or a tea towel until ready to serve.

To make the kebabs, put the lamb, onion, salt, marjoram, mint, baharat and loomi, if using, into a large bowl. Mix well with your hands. Form into 12 egg shapes and push onto skewers. Alternatively, shape the lamb around the skewers. Put the kebabs onto a lightly greased rack under a preheated grill and cook for about 8 minutes or until done. Alternatively, prepare a barbecue and brush the rack with a little oil so that the kebabs don't stick. Grill at medium heat for 5 minutes or until nicely browned, turning frequently to cook evenly.

Guests can assemble the kebabs themselves – use the flatbread as a base, add shallots and mint, then the kebabs, yoghurt mixture and sumac, if using.

***Note** Loomi are dried limes, available in Middle Eastern stores. Most come from Oman, and are used both whole and in powdered form throughout the Gulf States. Traditionally, limes are buried in the sand for a few months to dry or can be dried in the sun for at least a week. The spice is difficult to emulate, but you can omit it. You could, however, try drying a few pierced limes in the oven (which takes ages!) or the microwave. When dried, you can grind them to a powder.

main courses

- coriander
- sweet pimentón
- cumin

moroccan grilled fish
with chermoula spice paste

4 steaks of tuna, marlin or swordfish, about 200 g each, lightly scored

sea salt

olive oil, for grilling

coriander leaves, to serve

chermoula

a few handfuls of fresh coriander leaves and stems, coarsely chopped

3 garlic cloves, chopped

¼ teaspoon sweet pimentón (Spanish oak-smoked paprika)

½ teaspoon ground cumin

½ teaspoon chilli powder

4 tablespoons extra virgin olive oil

freshly squeezed juice of ½ lemon

sea salt

a ridged stove-top grill pan

serves 4

Chermoula is a spicy Moroccan sauce or marinade for fish. In dilapidated but bustling Tangier, huge baskets of spices and herbs, such as the coriander and cumin for chermoula, are lined up for sale in the souks. The colour of this sauce is produced by fresh coriander, while the chilli powder gives it a kick. It can be used as both a marinade and a topping.

To make the chermoula, put the coriander and garlic into a food processor or blender. Add the pimentón, cumin, chilli powder, olive oil, lemon juice and a pinch of salt and blend to a smooth paste – if necessary, add a dash of water to keep the blades turning. Alternatively, use a mortar and pestle.

About 30 minutes before cooking the fish, sprinkle it with salt, put a spoonful of chermoula onto each steak and rub all over. Set aside to marinate.

When ready to cook, brush a stove-top grill pan with olive oil and heat over medium-high heat until very hot. Add the fish and cook for 1–2 minutes, depending on the thickness of the fish steak. Don't move the fish until it loosens and will move without sticking. Turn it over and continue cooking for 1–2 minutes more. If the fish is very thick, cook for 1 minute longer, but do not overcook or the flesh will be tough. (If you have a small pan, cook in batches of 1 or 2 and keep them warm in a very low oven while you cook the remainder.)

Top each piece of fish with the remaining chermoula and serve with extra coriander leaves.

Note If you would like to serve the fish with typical North African accompaniments, roast some butternut squash or sweet potatoes with olive oil and cinnamon, and soak some fluffy couscous, with a little saffron added to the soaking water.

fish in a fennel salt crust

2 lemons

1 kg snapper or sea bream, scaled and cleaned

plenty of fennel stalks, foliage and flowers

250 g grey sea salt

250 g sea salt flakes

serves 2

Fennel is a pretty herb to grow, but if you don't have any, you can use the tops from a bulb of Florence fennel. However, this recipe works best with the whole plant – stalks, foliage and flowers. The salt forms a crust which keeps the fish moist. It does not make the fish very salty, because the crust is removed before serving, but it does somehow enhance the flavour of the sea. Serve with a simple salsa of finely chopped tomato, parsley and onion mixed with olive oil.

Cut 1 lemon into slices and use to stuff the cavity of the fish. Reserve a handful of fennel, and stuff the rest into the cavity.

Put the grey salt and salt flakes in a bowl and mix well. Put half the mixture in an ovenproof dish and shake to level. Arrange the fish in a single layer, then pack the remaining salt over the fish. Insert the remaining fennel into the salt.

Bake in a preheated oven at 200°C (400°F) Gas 6 for 15–20 minutes or until cooked. To test, insert a skewer through the salt into the fish – if it comes out very hot, the fish is done.

Crack open the crust and remove most of the salt. Serve with the remaining lemon cut into wedges.

- garlic
- flat leaf parsley
- coriander

hake in green sauce

12 mussels

16 clams

90 ml cava sparkling wine

4 hake steaks cut through the bone, about 200 g each (leave the bone in)

150 ml olive oil

4 garlic cloves, thinly sliced

1 tablespoon finely chopped flat leaf parsley, plus extra sprigs to serve

1 tablespoon finely chopped coriander leaves

sea salt

serves 4

Hake is a favourite fish in Spain, but is becoming seriously overfished, so feel free to substitute other white fish, such as haddock or ling. As it cooks, the fish gives out white juices, which you shake to form an emulsion with the oil. Wine and chopped herbs turn this emulsion into a wonderfully delicious green sauce. This dish is usually cooked in a flameproof earthenware *cazuela*, a flat cooking dish that retains heat well, although a heavy enamelled non-stick frying pan is equally good.

Put the mussels, clams and wine in a saucepan and cook over high heat. As the shellfish open, remove them to a bowl and cover with clingfilm. Discard any that fail to open. Strain the cooking juices through a muslin-lined sieve and set aside.

Put the hake on a plate and sprinkle with a little salt 10 minutes before cooking.

Put the olive oil and garlic in a heavy-based frying pan and heat gently so the garlic turns golden slowly and doesn't burn. Remove the garlic with a slotted spoon and keep until ready to serve.

Pour about two-thirds of the olive oil into a jug and add the hake to the oil left in the pan. Cook over very low heat moving the pan in a circular motion – keep taking it off the heat so it doesn't cook too quickly (the idea is to encourage the oozing of the juices instead of letting them fry and burn). Add the remaining oil little by little as you move the pan, so an emulsion starts to form. When all the oil has been added, remove the fish to a plate and keep it warm. Put the pan on the heat, add the reserved clam juices and stir to form the sauce.

Return the fish to the pan, add the chopped parsley and coriander and continue to cook until the fish is cooked, about 5 minutes. Just before serving, add the opened mussels, clams and fried garlic to the pan to heat through.

- chilli
- lemongrass
- ginger
- kaffir lime leaves
- Vietnamese coriander (left)

fried bream thai-style

This recipe features two classic Thai ingredients, lemongrass and kaffir lime leaf. The lime leaf's Thai name is *makrut* – 'kaffir' is the Hindi word for a foreigner, perhaps reflecting the odd way the leaves grow in pairs. They are waxy and smooth, in contrast to the fruit, which has knobbly skin. Both leaf and zest have a wonderfully fragrant lime flavour.

8 red bream or snapper fillets, about 750 g
3 red chillies, deseeded and thinly sliced
2 stalks of lemongrass, trimmed and thinly sliced
8 pink Thai shallots or 2 regular shallots, thinly sliced
5 cm fresh ginger, peeled, thinly sliced and cut into matchsticks
6 kaffir lime leaves, rolled and thinly sliced
12–18 Vietnamese coriander
oil, for frying
6 limes, cut into wedges, to serve

marinade

2 garlic cloves, finely chopped
2 stalks of lemongrass, trimmed and thinly sliced
1 teaspoon coriander seeds
1 teaspoon Szechuan pepper
1 teaspoon finely ground star anise
1 teaspoon ground galangal (Laos powder)
½ teaspoon salt
½ teaspoon freshly ground black pepper

serves 4

Cut each fillet in half and slash each piece twice on the skin side.

To make the marinade, use a mortar and pestle to grind the ingredients to a fine paste. Rub the paste into the slashes and into the flesh side of the fish pieces, then let marinate for 30 minutes.

Meanwhile, fill a wok about one-third full with oil, heat to about 190°C (375°F), or until a piece of noodle puffs up immediately. Add the chillies, lemongrass, shallots, ginger and kaffir lime leaves and deep-fry until crispy – work in batches if necessary to ensure a crisp result. Remove from the wok and drain on kitchen paper. Deep-fry the Vietnamese coriander in the same way – the leaves are left whole and are fragile when crisp. Remove from the wok and drain on kitchen paper. Pour the oil into a heatproof container and let cool.

To cook the fish, wipe any excess marinade off the skin side. Put about 100 ml of the oil back into the wok and heat gently. Working in batches, fry the fish, flesh side down over medium heat, for 1 minute, then turn the pieces over and fry for 1 minute more. As each piece is cooked, remove from the wok and pile onto plates. Serve topped with the crispy lemongrass mixture, deep-fried Vietnamese coriander and lime wedges.

- chervil (left)
- flat leaf parsley
- black sesame seeds
- celery leaves

crisp-fried herbed halibut

with shoestring potatoes

750 g waxy potatoes, such as Belle de Fontenay

1 egg white

1 tablespoon milk

750 g halibut fillet, cut into 8 pieces

3 sprigs of chervil

3 sprigs of flat leaf parsley

100 g plain flour

1 teaspoon black sesame seeds

½ teaspoon chilli powder

sea salt and freshly ground white pepper

sunflower oil, for deep-frying

to serve

celery leaves

flat leaf parsley leaves

spicy ketchup, for dipping

an electric deep-fryer

serves 4

Celery leaf makes a delicious herb, and plants are often now available in pots from garden centres. Alternatively, you could also use the pale leaves growing inside an ordinary head of celery. Celery and flat leaf parsley leaves are perfect crisply fried, and curly parsley is also good. Chervil and parsley are used to flavour the coating on the fish.

Using a mandolin, cut the potatoes as thinly as possible into strips, then put into a bowl of cold water to rinse off the starch. Drain and dry well with kitchen paper.

Fill a deep-fryer with oil to the manufacturer's recommended level and heat to 180°C (350°F). Working in batches, fry the potatoes until golden, then drain on kitchen paper. Keep hot.

Put the egg white and milk in a bowl and mix well. Rub the fish pieces with the egg white mixture. Finely chop the leaves from the chervil and parsley.

Sift the flour into a bowl, then add the chopped chervil and parsley, the sesame seeds, chilli powder, salt and pepper.

Deep-fry the celery and parsley leaves – they spit like mad, but will be crisp as soon as the spitting stops. Remove and drain on kitchen paper. Dip the fish into the bowl of flour mixture to coat, and fry 2 pieces at a time for 2–3 minutes until just cooked. Drain on kitchen paper and serve with the fried leaves, ketchup and crisp shoestring potatoes.

- ground coriander
- curry leaves

konju masala

spiced coconut prawns

2 garlic cloves, chopped

3 cm fresh ginger, peeled and chopped

2 tablespoons sunflower, groundnut or coconut oil*

4 small tomatoes, skinned and chopped

2 teaspoons white vinegar (wine or malt)

500 g uncooked shelled tiger prawns

sea salt

freshly shaved coconut, to serve

masala paste

1 small onion, quartered

grated flesh of ½ coconut, fresh or frozen

2 black peppercorns

2 red chillies, deseeded

¼ teaspoon ground turmeric

2 teaspoons ground coriander

½ teaspoon black mustard seeds

tarka spice-fry

1 tablespoon sunflower, groundnut or coconut oil*

a few curry leaves*

a few red chillies, deseeded and sliced

serves 4

This recipe originates from Kerala, the long and fertile state in India's south-west. Kerala's thus-far unspoilt Malabar Coast has, for thousands of years, been a magnet for merchants and nations in search of Eastern spices. The streets of the spice quarter of the beautiful old port city of Cochin are lined with 'godowns', 19th-century spice warehouses, with delicious scents of ginger and cinnamon, pepper and cassia issuing from their cavernous doorways. Kerala, like most of South India, reveres the coconut, so this prawn and coconut recipe is a good example of its fine seafood dishes. Rice and pooris (South Indian breads) are delicious served with this dish.

Put all the masala ingredients into a food processor or blender and work into a thick paste, adding a dash of water to keep the blades turning if necessary. Remove and set aside.

Put the garlic and ginger into the clean food processor and grind to a paste. Alternatively, use a mortar and pestle.

Heat 2 tablespoons oil in a wok or frying pan. Add the garlic and ginger paste and fry for a few seconds. Add the masala paste and stir-fry until the paste leaves the sides of the pan, about 8–10 minutes. Add the tomatoes, vinegar, salt and 250 ml water. Bring to the boil, add the prawns, reduce the heat and cook for 2–3 minutes, until the prawns turn pink. Transfer to a serving bowl.

To prepare the tarka spice-fry, heat the oil in a small frying pan, add the curry leaves and chillies and fry for about 45 seconds or so (this is called 'tempering').

Pour the tempered tarka over the prawns, top with shaved coconut and serve.

***Notes** Edible grade coconut oil is sold in many Indian shops and is popular in Kerala, the 'Land of Coconuts'. Curry leaves are always best fresh, and are often available in Indian or South-east Asian markets. Fresh ones may be frozen. If absolutely necessary, dried ones may be used instead. Please note that curry leaves are not related to the grey curry plant grown in some herb gardens.

- cumin
- fenugreek
- coriander (left)

coriander chicken with fenugreek

murgh methi

6 skinless, boneless chicken thighs
1 teaspoon cumin seeds, freshly ground
4 tablespoons sunflower oil
1 onion, finely chopped
5 garlic cloves, crushed
5 cm fresh ginger, grated
4 green chillies, deseeded and chopped, plus extra to serve
½ teaspoon ground turmeric
2 teaspoons coriander seeds, freshly ground
½ teaspoon fenugreek seeds, toasted in a dry frying pan, then ground
400 ml coconut milk
leaves from a bunch of fenugreek, about 30 g, or a pinch of ground fenugreek
leaves from a bunch of fresh coriander, about 30 g, plus extra sprigs, to serve
50 g roasted flaked almonds, toasted in a dry frying pan
sea salt and freshly ground black pepper
Indian breads, such as pooris, or rice, to serve

a large flameproof casserole

serves 4

The seeds of the fenugreek or methi plant are a common Indian spice. The leaves of the plant are sold in Indian and Middle Eastern greengrocers, and the spice seeds in the spice section of many supermarkets. In fact, they are what gives curry powder its distinctive aroma. Nothing compares with the astringently aromatic flavour of the fresh leaves and, if you have a garden, it's definitely worth growing yourself. However, when you buy the leaves, make sure they are fresh and perky – don't keep them too long in water, because they will lose their flavour. If you can't buy fresh fenugreek, this recipe is also good with just the fresh coriander leaves and ground fenugreek seeds.

Cut the chicken into large pieces, season with salt, pepper and ground cumin and set aside for 15 minutes at room temperature to develop the flavours.

Heat 2 tablespoons of the oil in a large flameproof casserole, add the chicken pieces and fry until golden. Using a slotted spoon, remove to a plate. Heat the remaining oil in the casserole, add the onion and fry until softened and translucent, about 7 minutes. Add the garlic, ginger and chillies, increase the heat and add the turmeric, coriander seeds and fenugreek seeds. Stir in 250 ml of the coconut milk and heat to simmering. Return the chicken pieces to the casserole and cover with the lid. Cook in a preheated oven at 190°C (375°F) Gas 5 for 20 minutes.

Put the fenugreek leaves and coriander leaves in a food processor or blender, add the remaining coconut milk and blend to a purée. Add to the chicken and cook for a further 5–10 minutes. Top with coriander sprigs, almonds and extra chilli, if using, and serve with Indian pooris or rice.

- ginger
- cinnamon
- star anise
- cloves

red-cooked chicken legs
with star anise

150 ml dark soy sauce
3 tablespoons Chinese rice wine or dry sherry
2 thin slices of fresh ginger
3 cinnamon sticks, halved
5 whole star anise
2 whole cloves
3 spring onions
½ teaspoon grated orange or lemon zest
1 tablespoon freshly squeezed lemon juice
½ teaspoon sugar
4 large chicken legs (thighs and drumsticks)

serves 4

Chinese red-cooking involves poaching meat, poultry, game, offal or even fish in a dark, soy-based sauce. When the sauce is spiced with star anise, cinnamon and other additional spices from the five-spice brigade, it is used as a 'master sauce'. You will sometimes find flavourings such as liquorice root and citrus peel in a master sauce as well, depending on the dish. Master sauce is used like a stock, cooked first as in the recipe below, then stored for later use in the refrigerator or freezer. When it has been used a few times, it is considered mature and more desirable. Serve with rice or a noodle dish, stir-fried vegetables and other Chinese dishes.

Pour the soy sauce and rice wine into a large saucepan and add 1 litre water. Add the ginger, cinnamon, star anise, cloves, spring onions, orange or lemon zest, lemon juice and sugar. Bring to the boil and turn off the heat. Leave for at least 10 minutes to infuse the flavours.

Add the chicken legs and bring to the boil. Reduce the heat and simmer for 40 minutes, or until cooked through and tender.

Transfer the chicken legs to a serving bowl or plate and spoon over some of the sauce. Alternatively, use a Chinese cleaver to chop them into bite-sized pieces. Transfer any remaining sauce to an airtight container and refrigerate (or freeze) for later use.

Note When cooking 'red' or master-sauce based recipes, it is important to get the right balance of liquids, or the sauce can be too strong. Regular soy sauce often contains wheat products: if you prefer wheat-free ingredients, use Japanese tamari soy sauce.

jerk chicken

4 chicken legs (thigh and drumstick)
1 recipe Jerk Seasoning Paste (page 172)*

to serve

lemon or lime wedges
soft buttered baps or rolls

serves 4

There are as many jerk chicken recipes in Jamaica as there are cooks, but all include the fiery Scotch bonnet chilli or the closely related habanero, plus a good dose of native allspice. Jerk seasoning also includes nutmeg, a native of the Spice Islands of Indonesia and grown in the West Indies since the 19th century. Today, jerk huts along the beaches are a magnet for tourists. Traditionally grilled over wood, jerk chicken – or pork – can easily be cooked on the barbecue or in the oven.

Cut slashes in the chicken legs and spread with half the jerk seasoning paste. Rub the paste all over and into the slashes, then cover and marinate in the refrigerator for at least 2 hours or overnight.

Put the chicken legs, skin side down, in a roasting tin. Roast in a preheated fan oven at 200°C (400°F) Gas 6 for 40–45 minutes or until crisp and cooked through, turning halfway through the cooking time and coating with the remaining marinade. (If using a regular oven, adjust the cooking time and temperature according to the manufacturer's instructions.)

Alternatively, preheat a charcoal grill until very hot. Cook the chicken over high heat to begin with, then adjust the rack further away from the fire as soon as the surfaces of the chicken have begun to brown. Cook for 15–20 minutes or until done, turning frequently and basting with the remaining marinade. You must cook poultry thoroughly so there is no pink inside: if you have an instant-read thermometer, it should read 75°C (165°F) when inserted into the thickest part of the thigh.

Serve hot with lemon or lime wedges and soft buttered baps or small rolls.

***Note** Jerk seasoning includes native Caribbean allspice and nutmeg brought from the Spice Islands of Indonesia. Allspice is a dried red berry, said to be redolent of nutmeg, cinnamon and cloves, hence 'all-spice'. It has a special fragrance, and is popular in the cooking of some European countries, such as Britain and Denmark, with former colonies in the West Indies. Nutmeg was smuggled out of the Spice Islands, breaking the Dutch stranglehold on its trade, and has been grown in the Caribbean since the 19th century.

- bouquet garni
- quatre épices spice mix

chicken quatre épices

25 g unsalted butter

2 tablespoons olive oil

1.5 kg free-range or organic chicken, cut into 8 pieces (breast portions halved)

1 celery stalk, chopped, with a few celery leaves reserved for the bouquet garni

½ large leek, chopped into thick chunks

1 onion, quartered

2 garlic cloves

12 baby carrots, 4 whole, 8 halved lengthways

a bouquet garni (a bunch of herbs, such as bay leaf, parsley, celery leaves and thyme, tied together with kitchen string)

1 teaspoon Quatre Epices (page 173)

1–1½ tablespoons cornflour

150 ml single cream (optional)

sea salt

aromatic stock

500 g chicken bones and wings

3 bay leaves

½ cinnamon stick

8 whole cloves

1 onion, halved, with roots still attached

sea salt

a flameproof casserole

serves 4

France's quatre épices, or 'four spices', is a popular blend of cloves, nutmeg, cinnamon and pepper. Sometimes ginger or allspice may also appear. Quatre épices is used with chicken and pork in stews and terrines. France has a love of aromatics – think of saffron in bouillabaisse, juniper berries with meats, especially pork, cloves in onions (as in this stock) and vanilla in puddings and pâtisserie. The flavour of this dish comes from the aromatic homemade stock (which can be made in advance), slow cooking, subtle spicing and delicate herbs – real comfort food.

To make the aromatic stock, put the chicken bones, bay leaves and cinnamon into a large saucepan. Stick the cloves into the onion and add to the pan, then cover with 2 litres water. Bring to the boil and skim off any foam. Reduce the heat to low, part-cover with a lid and let simmer very gently for 1–1½ hours. Strain through a fine-meshed sieve, let cool slightly, then skim off the globules of fat by trailing a small piece of kitchen paper across the surface. Add salt to taste.

Melt the butter and oil in a flameproof casserole and add the chicken pieces, celery, leek, onion, garlic and the 4 whole carrots. Turn to coat with the butter and cook for several minutes. Add stock to cover (about 650 ml); you can freeze any remaining stock for other dishes.

Add the bouquet garni and quatre épices, bring to the boil, then cover and cook in a preheated fan oven at 170°C (325°F) Gas 3 for 20 minutes. (If using a regular oven, adjust the cooking time and temperature according to the manufacturer's instructions.) Add the halved baby carrots and cook for a further 20–25 minutes or until the chicken is tender. To test, pierce with a skewer – the juices should run clear with no hint of pink. If not, simmer for a little longer.

Remove from the oven, carefully strain off the liquid into a saucepan, and skim off the fat. Bring the liquid to the boil and reduce by about half. Meanwhile, put the cornflour in a small cup and stir in a little water until smooth and lump-free. Add a little of the hot stock and stir immediately until smooth. Take the saucepan off the heat and whisk in the cornflour paste. Replace over low heat, whisking constantly. As the sauce is simmering, whisk in the cream, if using. Simmer, whisking a little, until the sauce has slightly thickened. Gently stir the sauce into the casserole. Discard the bouquet garni, reheat the casserole without boiling, then serve.

• hyssop

breast of guinea fowl
stuffed with hyssop and goats' cheese

1 tablespoon olive oil
4 guinea fowl breasts, with wing bone only left in and skin on
150 g firm goats' cheese, rind removed
4 sprigs of hyssop or lemon thyme
2 tablespoons thick honey
6 teaspoons orange flower water or rosewater
sea salt and freshly ground black pepper
mixed soft leaf herbs and flower salad, to serve

a shallow ovenproof dish

serves 4

Hyssop is still used today in Bedouin cooking. A native of the Mediterranean, it comes with pink or blue flowers which, like all herb flowers, are pretty in salads and for sprinkling over other dishes. It has a sweet anise flavour with slightly minty undertones. It can be quite pungent depending on the time of year, so just add a little at a time to see how you like it. If you can't get hold of any hyssop, try using one of the thymes, perhaps lemon- or orange-scented thyme.

Heat the olive oil in a large frying pan, add the guinea fowl skin side down and sear the skin until golden. Remove from the pan and carefully cut a pocket in each breast to contain the filling.

To make the filling, put the goats' cheese and hyssop in a bowl, then add 1 tablespoon of the honey, 2 teaspoons of the orange flower water, salt and pepper and mash well. Use to stuff the pockets in the guinea fowl breasts.

Arrange the guinea fowl breasts in the ovenproof dish. Mix the remaining orange flower water with 75 ml water and pour over the breasts. Poach in a preheated oven at 200°C (400°F) Gas 6 for 25 minutes until cooked.

Remove from the oven, put the breasts on a plate and cover with aluminium foil. Keep in a warm place for 8 minutes. Transfer the juices to a small saucepan and reduce over medium heat until reduced by one-third. Stir in the remaining honey to make a syrup.

To serve, cut the breasts diagonally, then transfer to warmed plates, trickle the syrup over the top and serve with a pretty herb and flower salad.

- garlic
- cayenne pepper
- basil
- coriander

rich lamb stew

with basil and coriander

4 tablespoons olive oil

750 g lamb neck fillets or boneless leg of lamb, cut into 2-cm chunks

2 large onions, chopped

2 garlic cloves, crushed

2 sweet red ramiro peppers, deseeded and chopped

4 ripe tomatoes, skinned, deseeded and coarsely chopped

½ teaspoon cayenne pepper

250 ml fresh vegetable stock or water

10 prunes

10 dried apricots

100 g okra, trimmed

2 Granny Smith apples, peeled, cored and cubed

400 g canned chickpeas, drained and rinsed

1 pomegranate, halved

a bunch of basil

a bunch of coriander

sea salt and freshly ground black pepper

a large ovenproof casserole

serves 6–8

This is a version of *bozbash*, an Armenian rich lamb stew, packed with herbs and fruity delicious flavours and textures. Neck fillet is ideal as it cooks quickly to tenderness due to the small amount of fat running through it. Pomegranates are a typical ingredient in Armenian cooking – sweet yet tart, with glorious colour, but you can leave them out if they're not in season. Potatoes are usually cooked in the stew, but baked potatoes topped with melted butter make a delicious accompaniment and give a contrast in texture. The herbs must be added at the last moment to keep their aromatic freshness.

Heat a large ovenproof casserole over high heat, add 2 tablespoons of the oil, then add the lamb in batches and brown on all sides. Remove to a plate, add 1 tablespoon of oil to the casserole, add the onions, garlic and red peppers and fry gently over low heat for 10 minutes.

Increase the heat and add the tomatoes and cayenne and cook until bubbling, about 5 minutes. Add the browned lamb, the stock, salt and pepper and bring to a gentle simmer. Cover with a lid and cook in a preheated oven at 200°C (400°F) Gas 6 for 20–30 minutes until just softening. Add the prunes and apricots and cook for a further 10 minutes.

Heat the remaining 1 tablespoon of oil in a frying pan, add the okra and apple and fry for 5 minutes. Transfer the okra, apple and chickpeas to the casserole and cook for 10 minutes. Test the meat for tenderness. If not yet done, lower the oven to 180°C (350°F) Gas 4 and cook for a further 10 minutes. Just before serving, squeeze the juice from half the pomegranate and fold into the casserole. Coarsely chop the basil and coriander and fold half into the stew. Serve sprinkled with the remaining herbs and the seeds from the remaining pomegranate half.

- ground turmeric
- ground ginger
- ras el hanout spice mix

lamb and apricot tagine

½ teaspoon ground turmeric

½ teaspoon ground ginger

1 kg boned shoulder of lamb, well trimmed of fat and cut into large chunks

25 g unsalted butter

2 onions, chopped

½ cinnamon stick

1 tablespoon Ras el Hanout (page 174)

1 tomato, skinned and chopped, or 2 tablespoons chopped canned tomatoes

1 teaspoon honey (optional)

175 g dried apricots, halved

sea salt

to serve

steamed couscous

a few coriander leaves

2 tablespoons sesame seeds, toasted in a dry frying pan

1–2 tablespoons argan oil (optional)*

serves 4

Used in North African cooking, ras el hanout is one of the most intricate spice blends – and all the more alluring for its mystery. Moroccan spice merchants blend their own secret recipes, adding all manner of spices, flower petals, roots, bark and aphrodisiacs like Spanish fly! Unusual spices, such as cubeb, grains of paradise, monk's pepper, ash berries, long pepper, galangal and nigella, are sometimes included. A tagine is a slow-cooked stew that takes its name from the conical earthenware pot in which it is traditionally cooked. Avoid the urge to raise the heat and cook the lamb quickly, as the slow simmering over low heat is key to the tagine's tenderness and the reduction of the sauce.

A few hours before making the tagine, put the turmeric and ginger into a bowl, mix well, then rub into the lamb. Cover and set aside to develop the flavours.

Melt the butter in a heavy-based saucepan or casserole and add the onions, cinnamon, lamb, ras el hanout and salt. Mix well, then add the tomato, honey, if using, and 475 ml water. Bring to the boil, then reduce the heat to low and simmer gently, part-covered with a lid, for 45 minutes, stirring occasionally. Uncover and simmer for a further 45 minutes, stirring occasionally.

Add the apricots and continue to simmer gently for 25 minutes. When ready, the sauce should just coat the lamb all over, rich and almost glaze-like. Remove from the heat. Serve hot with couscous and sprinkle with coriander leaves, sesame seeds and a little argan oil, if using.

***Note** Argan oil is extracted from the nuts of Morocco's argan tree, and is said to be even healthier than the best olive oil. The trees, once common, have been dying out, but efforts are now being made to re-establish them. The oil is expensive because it takes 30 kg of nuts to produce 1 litre. It is used in dips, on its own or in dressings. It is sometimes available in specialist shops and is definitely worth trying if you see it for sale.

- garlic
- chilli
- cardamom (left)
- cinnamon

spicy lamb in almond milk

badami elachi gosht

Rich and creamy and steeped in plenty of almond and cardamom sauce, this 'white' dish is a refined affair, like many a Moghul recipe developed for kings and courtiers. The wet paste of garlic, chillies, almonds and onions provides body and is typical of northern Indian cooking (although this combination is popular in other parts of India, too). The cardamom and cinnamon scent the butter or ghee before other ingredients are added. White pepper is classically used in this dish, in keeping with its colour.

2 tablespoons unsalted butter or ghee (clarified butter)

5 green cardamom pods, bruised

½ cinnamon stick

1¼ kg leg of lamb, well trimmed, boned and cut into chunks, or 800 g boned

5 tablespoons natural yoghurt, whisked

¼ teaspoon cardamom seeds (not pods)

325 ml double cream

sea salt

wet paste

2 large garlic cloves, sliced

1½ large onions, quartered

4 green chillies, deseeded and coarsely chopped

5 tablespoons ground almonds

to serve

freshly ground white pepper

thinly sliced red onion, soaked in a little vinegar

unroasted flaked almonds

Perfumed Persian Pulow (page 132) or boiled basmati rice

naan bread

light Indian vegetable side dishes, such as Rato Farshi or Mattar Paneer (page 117)

serves 4–6

To make the wet paste, put the garlic, onions, chillies and almonds into a food processor or blender and blend until smooth, adding a little water to keep the blades turning if necessary. Alternatively, use a mortar and pestle. Set aside.

Melt the butter in a large, heavy-based saucepan and add the cardamom pods and cinnamon. Let the spices flavour the butter for 1–2 minutes, then add the wet paste. Sauté the paste for 8 minutes until thickened, stirring frequently to avoid burning.

Add the lamb and stir-fry until brown. Then add the yoghurt and enough water to cover, 250–325 ml, and whisk well. Heat until almost boiling, stirring constantly. Part-cover with a lid, then reduce the heat to low and simmer very gently for 45 minutes. (Lamb cooked over low heat becomes very tender.)

Remove the lid, then stir in the cardamom seeds and salt. Cook for 30 minutes longer. (The sauce may look slightly separated, but don't worry.)

Finally, stir in the cream, increase the heat and bring to the boil. Reduce the heat and simmer gently for a few minutes to let the sauce thicken slightly. Sprinkle with white pepper, sliced red onion and a few flaked almonds. Serve with perfumed Persian pulow, naan bread and vegetable side dishes.

- chilli
- bay leaves (left)
- garlic
- coriander

portuguese pork and clams with bay leaves

750 g pork shoulder steaks
150 ml extra virgin olive oil
about ¼ teaspoon sea salt
1 onion, finely chopped
100 ml white wine
500 g potatoes, cut into 1.5-cm cubes
a handful of coriander leaves, chopped, plus extra sprigs to serve
500 g fresh manila or venus clams, in the shell
sea salt and freshly ground black pepper
lemon wedges, to serve (optional)

marinade

2 tablespoons red sweet pepper cream (*crema di pepperoni*)*
1 tablespoon sweet paprika
1 chilli, deseeded and finely chopped
2 whole cloves
2 fresh bay leaves
5 garlic cloves, crushed

a large flameproof casserole

serves 4

Pork and clams – *carne de porco a Alentejana* – make this simple meal from southern Portugal, a region where bay, coriander and garlic richly flavour the dishes. Apart from Portugal and parts of Spain, coriander isn't a traditional herb in European cooking. Prepare this dish in advance, then steam open the clams and add herbs before serving.

To make the marinade, put the pepper cream, paprika, chilli, cloves, bay leaves and garlic in a glass or ceramic bowl. Cut the pork into large chunks and add to the bowl, then add 4 tablespoons of the olive oil and mix to coat the meat. Let marinate for 2 hours or overnight in the refrigerator.

30 minutes before cooking, remove the pork from the refrigerator and sprinkle with salt. When ready to cook, heat 1 tablespoon of the olive oil in the casserole, add the onion and fry for 7 minutes until softened but not coloured. Remove to a plate. Add 2 tablespoons more oil, then sear the meat in batches on both sides over high heat. As each is browned, transfer to a plate using a slotted spoon. Increase the heat, add the wine and boil hard for 30 seconds. Add the pork, salt and pepper, cover with a lid and cook in a preheated oven at 180°C (350°F) Gas 4 for 40 minutes. Remove the lid and cook, uncovered, for 5 minutes.

Just before serving, heat the remaining oil in a large frying pan, add the potatoes and fry until tender and golden on all sides. Keep them warm until ready to serve.

Put the clams in a saucepan with about 3 tablespoons of water. Cover with a lid, bring to the boil and cook until the clams open, about 3–4 minutes. Discard any that don't open. Remove the clams from the pan and strain the juices through a muslin-lined sieve set over a bowl. Add the juices to the casserole, then stir in the chopped coriander. Add the opened clams, potatoes and sprigs of coriander to the casserole and serve with lemon wedges, if liked.

Note *Crema di pepperoni* is a creamy red pepper sauce available from good delicatessens.

- chilli
- ginger
- galangal
- turmeric

burmese pork hinleh

This curry is a Burmese speciality and doesn't include the coconut milk so typical of South-east Asian cooking. It does use three root spices from the same family – turmeric, ginger and galangal. In Burma and throughout Asia, all three are used fresh, but in the West, turmeric is rarely available fresh, so the ground form must be used instead. If you can't get fresh galangal, use extra fresh ginger instead (a pity, because galangal's bright flavour is delicious).

3 tablespoons groundnut or vegetable oil

750 g well trimmed boneless pork sparerib, sliced into chunks*

500 ml beef stock

hinleh (curry) paste

4–6 red bird's eye chillies, deseeded and chopped

5 garlic cloves, quartered

½ onion, coarsely chopped

5 cm fresh ginger, peeled and grated

¼ teaspoon ground turmeric

2 cm fresh galangal, peeled and grated

1 stalk of lemongrass, outer leaves discarded, the remainder very finely chopped

3 anchovies in oil, drained and finely chopped, plus a dash of fish sauce, or ½ teaspoon toasted shrimp paste (see note, page 24)

to serve

a handful of Thai basil or coriander

2 red bird's eye chillies, thinly sliced lengthways

boiled rice

serves 4

To make the hinleh paste, put all the ingredients in a food processor or blender and grind to a paste, adding a dash of water to keep the blades turning if necessary. Alternatively, use a mortar and pestle.

Heat the oil in a large saucepan, then add the hinleh paste and stir-fry for several minutes. Add the pork and stir-fry to seal. Add the stock and bring to the boil, then reduce the heat and simmer gently, stirring occasionally, for 40–45 minutes until cooked through but very tender. Sprinkle with the Thai basil and chilli and serve with rice.

***Note** Boneless sparerib meat takes longer to cook, but doesn't dry out as easily as leg meat. It gives best results at a lower temperature. Otherwise, you can also use the best cut – fillet – for tender, fast cooking meat.

- fennel seeds (left)
- black pepper
- garlic

italian pork tenderloin

with fennel and garlic

2 free-range pork tenderloins, about 400–500 g each, trimmed

fennel and pepper seasoning

2 teaspoons fennel seeds

½ teaspoon coarse salt

5 black peppercorns

2 garlic cloves, crushed

6 tablespoons extra virgin olive oil

serves 4

The Romans had an insatiable desire for spices. They used native fennel and coriander seeds and 'exotic' spices such as black pepper. In his first-century cookbook, Apicius mentions spice mixtures using fennel seeds, and fennel was part of the reverse spice trade. The Romans probably introduced the seed to India (either directly or via Arab middlemen), where it is now much used. Today, fennel is found in the fine Tuscan sausage *finocchiona*, and is partnered with other sausages and pork all over Italy. Incidentally, the marriage of pork with spices, such as fennel or coriander, spread from Italy to England, proving especially popular during Elizabethan times.

There are two ways to cook the pork. If you're in a rush, use the fast-roast method, a favourite with many modern cooks. However, the slow-cooking method keeps meat like pork more moist and tender.

To make the fennel and pepper seasoning, grind the fennel seeds, salt and peppercorns with a mortar and pestle. Mash in the garlic and olive oil to form a paste. Make a few light slashes in each tenderloin and put on a baking sheet. Rub the seasoning oil all over the pork and pour any remaining oil on top.

To fast-roast the pork, cook on the middle shelf of a preheated fan oven at 220°C (425°F) Gas 7 for 20 minutes, or until the internal temperature registers 65°C (150°F) on an instant-read thermometer, or until there are no pink juices when you pierce the meat with a skewer. (If using a regular oven, adjust the cooking time and temperature according to the manufacturer's instructions.) Baste the pork several times while roasting.

If using the slow-cooking method, cook in a preheated fan oven at 170°C (325°F) Gas 3 for 45 minutes or until done, as above. Baste several times while roasting. For both methods, rest the pork for 10 minutes before slicing and serving.

- garlic
- oregano (left)
- purple basil
- green peppercorns

char-grilled steak

with basil and oregano salsa

6 thick sirloin steaks, about 1.5 kg total
sea salt and freshly ground black pepper
oil, for brushing

basil and oregano salsa

1 small shallot, chopped
3 garlic cloves, crushed
6 sprigs of oregano
a large bunch of purple basil
1 stalk of fresh green peppercorns, or 1 tablespoon green peppercorns preserved in brine
150 ml olive oil
1 tablespoon red wine vinegar
1 red chilli, deseeded and finely chopped

to serve

watercress
sprigs of purple basil

a ridged stove-top grill pan

serves 6

This salsa is a variation on chimichurri (page 102), which is usually made with parsley and served in individual small bowls with thick, rare char-grilled steaks. A big bowl of peppery fresh watercress makes an ideal accompaniment. Purple or 'opal' basil has a minty, oil-of-cloves quality to its flavour. The purple-black leaves become brighter and more intense in colour when plunged into hand-hot water – this will also revive a flopped bunch within 10 minutes. Oregano is widely used in Latin American cuisine to flavour sauces, salsas and meat dishes.

To make the basil and oregano salsa, pound the shallot and garlic to a coarse paste using a mortar and pestle.

Pull the leaves off the sprigs of oregano and purple basil and pound into the paste. Remove the green peppercorns from the stalk and pound them into the paste. Start adding the olive oil a little at a time, then pound in the vinegar and chilli, keeping the mixture chunky. Alternatively, put the salsa ingredients in a food processor or blender and pulse to make a coarse paste.

Brush the steaks with oil and season well with salt and pepper. Heat a ridged stove-top grill pan and, when it starts to smoke, add the steaks and cook for 1½–2 minutes on each side. Remove from the pan and let rest in a warm place for 5 minutes. Slice thickly and serve with the chimichurri, watercress and sprigs of purple basil.

- Thai red curry paste
- kaffir lime leaves
- Thai holy basil

thai beef curry with basil

pha naeng neua

750 g beef fillet
400 ml coconut milk
1–2 tablespoons Thai Red Curry Paste (page 179)
85 g peanuts, roasted and ground
2 tablespoons palm sugar
5 kaffir lime leaves
a bunch of Thai holy basil
3 tablespoons Thai fish sauce
freshly squeezed juice of ½ lime, or to taste

to serve

2 teaspoons sunflower oil
150 g beansprouts, rinsed, trimmed and drained
8 pink Thai shallots or 2 regular shallots, thinly sliced
2 mild green chillies, deseeded and sliced into rings (optional)*

serves 6

There are two kinds of Thai holy basil – the one with dark purple-tinged leaves, stalk and flower is the most fragrant when heated in curries and this is the variety used in meat curries. The leaves are more sturdy and, when you crush them between your fingers, they have a minty, almost camphor-like aroma. The lighter, paler, Thai holy basil has a softer, slightly hairy leaf with a distinct oily aroma. It is used in non-meat curries and noodle dishes. If you can't find either of these, sprinkle Thai sweet basil over the dish at the last moment.

Cut the beef in half lengthways, then into thin diagonal slices. Put half the coconut milk and the curry paste in a wok and heat slowly until just boiling. Add the rest of the milk and simmer gently for 5 minutes. Add the peanuts, palm sugar and kaffir lime leaves and simmer for a further 2 minutes. Strip the leaves from the holy basil and add to the wok, then add the fish sauce. Stir in the beef and cook for 1 minute to wilt the basil leaves and lightly cook the beef. Add lime juice to taste and divide between 6 deep bowls.

Heat the oil in a wok, add the beansprouts and stir-fry for 1 minute. Add to the bowls of curry, top with the shallots and chillies, if using, and serve immediately.

***Note** To deseed a chilli before slicing into rings, massage it between your thumb and forefinger until the seeds feel loose inside. Cut off the stalk end and bang the chilli on the work surface so all the seeds fall out. To cut the chilli into fine matchsticks, cut in half lengthways and remove the seeds with a teaspoon, then slice thinly.

- flat leaf parsley
- sweet pimentón

argentine barbecued beef

with chimichurri

4 sirloin or T-bone steaks

sea salt and freshly ground black pepper

olive oil, for brushing

chimichurri

75 g fresh flat leaf parsley, trimmed of tough stalks and coarsely chopped

2 large garlic cloves, quartered

½ teaspoon sweet pimentón (Spanish oak-smoked paprika)

¼ teaspoon freshly grated nutmeg

a pinch of ground cinnamon

a pinch of chilli powder or chilli flakes

2 tablespoons freshly squeezed lemon juice

150 ml extra virgin olive oil or corn oil

sea salt, to taste

dressing

½ small onion, finely chopped

¾ teaspoon caster sugar

1 teaspoon freshly squeezed lemon juice

1 red pepper, finely chopped (about 6 tablespoons)

¼ teaspoon freshly grated nutmeg

2 tablespoons extra virgin olive oil or corn oil

serves 4

Argentine beef is legendary, thanks to the seemingly endless grazing land of the pampas and the country's own brand of cowboys, the gauchos. These oft-romanticized characters have left a strong imprint on local food traditions. Beef is often cooked on a *parrilla* – a large barbecue grill – and served on its own or with condiments like chimichurri. Argentines have many versions of this parsley-based sauce/relish; some include nutmeg, cinnamon or cumin, while others are without spice. Chimichurri contains a native chilli, *aji molido*, which is unique in its mellow, sweet, smoky heat. Since it is rare in other parts of the world, this recipe uses Spanish sweet pimentón (oak-smoked paprika) instead, plus chilli flakes or powder. Serve the steaks with accompaniments such as barbecued vegetables and baked potatoes, which can be cooked in the coals.

To make the chimichurri, put all the ingredients in a food processor or blender and work to a smooth sauce. Alternatively use a mortar and pestle.

To make the dressing, put the onion in a bowl, add the sugar and lemon juice and stir well. Cover and set aside for at least 30 minutes. Add the pepper, nutmeg, olive oil and 3–4 tablespoons of the chimichurri. Mix well and set aside. (Save any remaining chimichurri base for use as a pesto-type topping, or pour into ice cube trays, freeze and use for flavouring stocks, soups and stews.)

To prepare the beef, preheat a charcoal grill until very hot (you can add oak or hickory chips if available) and brush the steaks with a little oil. Cook over a fierce heat to begin with, then adjust the rack further away from the fire as soon as the surfaces of the steaks have begun to sear. Cook to your liking, turning once. Alternatively, cook under a preheated grill or on a ridged stove-top grill pan. Sprinkle with salt and pepper, then serve hot with the chimichurri.

Variation For a more spicy chimichurri, mix in 1 finely choped poblano or other mild green chilli.

vegetable dishes

- garlic
- flat leaf parsley
- marjoram (left)

imam bayildi

4 large aubergines, with long stalks if possible, halved lengthways

200 ml extra virgin olive oil

500 g onions, halved and very thinly sliced

4 garlic cloves, crushed

750 g Italian plum tomatoes, skinned, deseeded and finely chopped

leaves from 15 sprigs of flat leaf parsley

leaves from 12 sprigs of marjoram

2 teaspoons sugar

1 small lemon, thinly sliced

sea salt and freshly ground black pepper

an ovenproof dish, big enough to hold the aubergines in a single layer

serves 4–8

This Middle Eastern aubergine dish literally means 'the priest fainted'. It got its name because the priest (the Imam) found it so delicious that he swooned. Some stories tell that he really fainted because he was horrified at the amount of oil used to cook it. This is the secret of course – aubergines must be cooked well, with large quantities of oil. It uses the heavily scented marjoram – when it has its knotted flowers in bloom, use those, too – and lots of parsley.

Cut a line 5 mm in from the edges of the aubergine halves, then score the flesh inside with a criss-cross pattern. Rub plenty of olive oil all over the aubergines and season with a little salt. Arrange in a single layer in the ovenproof dish. Cook in a preheated oven at 200°C (400°F) Gas 6 for about 30 minutes or until the flesh has just softened.

Heat 75 ml of the oil in a heavy-based frying pan, add the onions and garlic, cover with a lid and cook over low heat until soft. Increase the heat and add the tomatoes. Cook until the juices from the tomatoes have reduced a little, then add salt and pepper to taste. Reserve a few parsley leaves for serving, then chop the remainder together with the marjoram. Add to the onion and tomato mixture, then add the sugar.

Scoop some of the central flesh out of the aubergines, leaving a shell around the outside to hold the base in shape. Chop the scooped out section and add to the tomato mixture. Pile the mixture into the aubergine shells and sprinkle with pepper. Arrange the lemon slices on top. Trail more oil generously over the top, then sprinkle with 4 tablespoons of water.

Cover with aluminium foil and bake for 30–40 minutes until meltingly soft. Remove the foil about 10 minutes before the end. Serve, sprinkled with any remaining oil and the reserved parsley.

- sage
- chilli

sage buttered baby leeks
with chilli breadcrumbs

75 g salted butter

2 tablespoons finely chopped sage

500 g short thin baby leeks, split halfway through and well washed

2 tablespoons extra virgin olive oil

50 g fresh ciabatta breadcrumbs

1 mild long red chilli, deseeded and finely chopped

1 smaller red chilli, deseeded and sliced into rings

serves 4

Sage makes a great partnership with leeks, and the Italian-style chilli breadcrumb topping makes for a delicious combination. For an even more pronounced Italian accent, the crispy breadcrumbs are made from ciabatta bread. If possible, use the mild, tender leaves of the gold variegated sage, *Salvia officinalis* 'Icterina', for a less 'thuggish' medicinal flavour.

Put the butter and sage in a bowl and mash well.

Steam or boil the leeks for about 5 minutes, or until tender. Toss in half the sage butter and keep hot.

Heat a frying pan, add the olive oil and ciabatta breadcrumbs and fry for about 45 seconds. Add the remaining sage butter and the finely chopped chillies. Fry until golden.

Put the leeks on a serving plate, and top with the chilli breadcrumbs and the smaller sliced chilli. Serve with other dishes or as a starter.

Note Sea kale and salsify are also good served this way.

- garlic
- lovage (left)
- thyme

artichokes provençal

1 lemon, halved
18–24 baby artichokes, depending on size
3 tablespoons extra virgin olive oil
200 g smoked bacon pieces (lardons)
300 g small shallots
3 garlic cloves, halved
4 carrots, halved lengthways and cut into fine strips
200 ml white wine
100 ml vegetable stock
2 young sprigs of lovage, or a few celery leaves
a large sprig of thyme
200 g cooked flageolet or cannellini beans
sea salt and freshly ground black pepper

to serve

crusty bread
boiled red Camargue rice
salad leaves

a heavy, shallow flameproof casserole

serves 6

This dish is based on a dish from Provence, where the violet artichokes are picked before the hairy choke has formed. This recipe uses lovage, thyme and beans, cooked in a shallow terracotta dish. Only a small amount of lovage is needed to give maximum flavour. If you've never tasted it, prepare to be smitten – it's a delightful herb, full of character, similar to celery in some ways.

Squeeze the cut lemon halves into a bowl of cold water and add the lemon shells. Set aside to add the artichokes as they are prepared (the acidulated water will prevent them from discolouring).

To prepare the artichokes, remove about 3 layers of tough leaves from the outside, cut off the top 1 cm of the leaves and trim the stalks to about 3 cm. Using a vegetable peeler, peel the stalks. As you work, add the artichokes to the bowl of lemon water.

Heat 1 tablespoon of olive oil in the casserole, add the bacon and fry until crisp and golden. Transfer to a plate.

Add the remaining oil to the casserole, then fry the whole shallots and garlic until golden. Drain the artichokes, then add them to the casserole. Add the carrots and stir-fry for 2 minutes. Add the wine, bring to the boil and let reduce for 2 minutes. Add the stock and simmer for 2 minutes, then add the lovage, thyme, salt and pepper.

Cover and cook in a preheated oven at 200°C (400°F) Gas 6 for 20 minutes until the artichokes are tender. Add the beans, return to the oven and heat through, uncovered, for 5 minutes. Serve with bread, boiled rice and salad.

- garlic
- rosemary
- bay leaves (left)

oven-roasted vegetables

with rosemary, bay leaves and garlic

500 g ratte or other salad potatoes, cut into 5-cm chunks

about 500 g butternut squash, cut into wedges and deseeded

6 small red onions, quartered

4 tablespoons extra virgin olive oil

8 garlic cloves, unpeeled

2 red romano (long) peppers, deseeded and cut into chunks

4 sprigs of rosemary

4 sprigs of bay leaves

sea salt

serves 4

Roasted vegetables are made extra special with the strong flavours of herbs. Rosemary is delicious with roasted vegetables, although it should be used sparingly as too much can overwhelm a dish. Thyme also works well in this dish. Bay leaves are quite mild when young, so don't use as many if you have mature leaves.

Bring a large saucepan of water to the boil, add salt and the potatoes and cook for 5 minutes. Drain, then put in a large roasting tin. Add the squash, onions and 2 tablespoons of the olive oil. Toss to coat, then roast in a preheated oven at 200°C (400°F) Gas 6 for 10 minutes.

Add 1 extra tablespoon of oil to the roasting tin, followed by the garlic and peppers, 2 sprigs of rosemary and 2 sprigs of bay leaves. Roast for 15 minutes, then add the rest of the herbs and continue roasting for 10–15 minutes. Turn the vegetables occasionally until they are all tender and the edges slightly charred. Trail the remaining oil over the top, then serve.

Variation Sprinkle the vegetables with 3 tablespoons of pine nuts and some crumbled feta cheese 5 minutes before the end of the cooking time, so that the nuts roast a little and the feta softens.

• mint
• ajowan seeds

indian vegetarian fritters

bondas, pakoras or wadas

½ large cucumber, cut crossways into thick slices

½ large cauliflower, broken into florets

groundnut or sunflower oil, for deep-frying

batter*

225 g chickpea flour (called gram flour or besan in Asian shops and farina de ceci in Italian delicatessens)

½ teaspoon ajowan seeds (optional)

½ teaspoon cumin seeds

a large pinch of chilli powder

1 teaspoon salt

green chutney

2 handfuls of mint leaves, chopped

1 handful of fresh coriander, chopped

2 green chillies, chopped

freshly squeezed juice of ½ lemon

a pinch of salt

thick natural yoghurt (not low-fat; optional)

to serve

chutneys or Indian pickles

lemon wedges

serves 4–6

see note on dough and batter, page 4

Bondas, pakodas or pakoras, and wadas are all favourite street food in the Indian subcontinent. These deep-fried vegetable snacks go well with Indian chutneys (savoury or sweet). Many Indian chutneys are made with fresh herbs, rather than the sweet chutneys with which most people in the West are familiar. You can also serve Indian pickles (you'll find an interesting selection in Indian stores).

To make the green chutney, put the mint, coriander, chillies, lemon juice and salt into a blender and blend to a purée, adding water to keep the blades turning. Serve as is, or stir in the yoghurt.

To make the batter, put the chickpea flour into a large bowl and add the spices and salt. Mix with a fork, breaking up any lumps. Add enough water (a little at a time) to make a thick, smooth batter, whisking to achieve the right consistency. The batter should be thick enough to coat and cling to the vegetables.

Heat the oil in a deep saucepan to 190°C (375°F) or until a cube of bread turns brown in 30 seconds. Dip a cucumber slice into the batter and coat well. Using tongs, carefully slide it into the oil. Fry in batches without overcrowding the pan, for a few minutes until golden, turning them several times. As each piece is done, lift it out with a slotted spoon or tongs and drain in a colander lined with kitchen paper. As soon as one batch is drained, transfer the pieces to a platter and keep them warm in a low oven until all are cooked. When all the cucumber has been fried, repeat with the cauliflower, which will take slightly longer to cook.

Serve with lemon wedges and a chutney or two of your choice.

Variation These fritters can be made with all sorts of vegetables and the spices can be varied too. Southern bondas use curry leaves and spices such as asafoetida and mustard seeds, while Bombay bondas or batat wadas may call for ginger, turmeric, chillies and garlic. Slices of aubergine, courgettes, green peppers or sliced or mashed potatoes also make good bondas, but with mashed potatoes, the spices are fried in oil and added to the mash rather than the batter.

rato farshi nepali pumpkin

- 1.25 kg pumpkin, peeled, deseeded and cut into medium chunks
- ½ teaspoon ground turmeric
- 2 tablespoons sunflower oil or ghee (clarified butter)
- ½ cinnamon stick
- 4–5 cardamom pods, bruised
- 1 onion, finely chopped
- 3 cm fresh ginger, peeled and grated
- 2 garlic cloves, crushed
- 150 ml canned chopped tomatoes
- 1½ heaped teaspoons ground cumin
- 1½ heaped teaspoons ground coriander
- ½ teaspoon sugar or jaggery (unrefined palm sugar)
- 75 ml single cream
- ¼ teaspoon ground white cardamom (seeds not pods), plus extra for dusting
- sea salt and freshly ground black pepper
- fresh coriander leaves, to serve

serves 4

Serve this aromatic side dish with other vegetable dishes and rice.

Put the pumpkin into a saucepan, cover with water, then add a pinch of salt and half the turmeric. Bring to the boil, reduce the heat and cook for about 12 minutes or until tender. Drain, reserving 75 ml of the cooking liquid and set aside. Freeze the remaining liquid for later use as a stock.

Heat the oil in a frying pan, then add the cinnamon, cardamom pods and remaining turmeric. Fry briefly until aromatic, taking care not to let the spices burn. Add the onion and sauté for about 6 minutes. Remove the cardamom and cinnamon and add the ginger and garlic. Sauté for a few more minutes over low heat, until the onion is very soft.

Add the tomatoes, pumpkin liquid, cumin and coriander. Mix well and cook until the tomatoes have boiled down to a thick sauce. Add the pumpkin and mash into the sauce until well blended. Continue to cook, stirring regularly, for 5–6 minutes until soft. Add the sugar, cream and ground cardamom. Cook for another minute. Taste and adjust the seasoning, then serve, sprinkled with coriander leaves.

mattar paneer peas & cheese

- 2 tablespoons groundnut oil or ghee
- 500 g paneer (2 blocks) or haloumi cheese, cubed*
- ¼ teaspoon ground turmeric
- ¼–½ teaspoon chilli powder
- 1 teaspoon cumin seeds
- 1 onion, finely chopped
- 400 g shelled peas, fresh or frozen
- 1–1½ teaspoons Punjabi Garam Masala (page 176)
- sea salt

to serve

- 2–3 red chillies, deseeded and sliced (optional)
- Indian breads, such as pooris, parathas or naan

serves 6

In India, the cheese is usually homemade, so you can either follow the recipe below or replace the paneer with haloumi.

Heat 1 tablespoon oil in a non-stick frying pan and swirl to coat. Add the paneer, sear for about 4 minutes or until brown, then turn and brown the other side. Remove from the pan and, when cool enough to handle, cut into cubes.

Heat the remaining oil in the pan. Add the turmeric, chilli powder and cumin seeds and sizzle briefly. Add the onions and sauté over low heat for 8 minutes or until soft. Add the peas, garam masala and salt and stir-fry for a few minutes, until the peas are cooked. Add the paneer cubes, mix and warm through. Top with the chillies, if using. Serve hot with Indian breads.

***Note** Paneer, sold in supermarkets or Indian shops, has a firm texture, ideal for frying and tandoori cooking. To make your own, put 2 tablespoons lemon juice and 1 litre milk into a bowl. Let set, then drain through muslin. Weigh down with a plate to make it firmer.

- Thai red curry paste
- kaffir lime leaves
- chilli
- basil

vegetable curry

gaeng ped pak

2 tablespoons groundnut or sunflower oil
2 tablespoons Thai Red Curry Paste (page 179)
600 ml coconut cream
600 ml vegetable stock
4 Chinese longbeans, cut into 2.5-cm pieces
4 carrots, cut into matchsticks
5 ears of baby corn, cut into 2.5-cm pieces
80 g cauliflower, cut into florets
4 kaffir lime leaves, coarsely chopped
2 large fresh red or green chillies, coarsely sliced
3 tablespoons light soy sauce
2 teaspoons sugar
½ teaspoon salt
6 small round green aubergines, quartered
30 fresh basil leaves
rice, to serve

serves 4

Curry originated in the Indian subcontinent and migrated eastwards long before it travelled west to Europe and North America. Over centuries, it has been adapted to local ingredients and tastes in several other Asian countries, notably Thailand, where many curries are considered to be even hotter and more flavoursome than their Indian cousins. Red curry paste is used as the core curry ingredient in many Thai dishes (see also Thai Green Chicken Curry, page 59).

Put the oil in a saucepan, heat well, then quickly stir in the curry paste. Add the coconut cream, mixing well. Add the vegetable stock and stir briefly.

Add the longbeans, carrots, corn, cauliflower, kaffir lime leaves, chillies, soy sauce, sugar, salt and aubergines. Stir well, then cook for a few minutes until the vegetables are cooked to your taste.

Add the basil leaves, stir once, then ladle into a bowl and serve with rice.

pasta, rice & bread

- flat leaf parsley (left)
- chilli

homemade herb pasta

with herb oil

200 g Italian 00 pasta flour or plain flour

2 large eggs (orange yolks will give a stronger pasta colour)

about 36 fresh herb leaves, such as chervil, flat leaf parsley or sweet cicely, or flowers such as marigolds and nasturtiums (make sure they aren't damp), plus extra to serve

about 200 g baby spinach

3 mild dried chillies, deseeded and ground with a pinch of salt

sea salt

homemade herb oil, such as basil or parsley, to serve (page 170)

a pasta machine

serves 4

Homemade herb pasta is fun to make with children – it's almost like paper making. If you have herbs growing in your garden, this is a wonderful way to use them. Pasta dough made with '00' pasta flour can be made 1 day ahead and kept in the refrigerator.

Put the flour and a pinch of salt in a food processor and pulse to mix. Put the eggs in a bowl and beat with a fork, then add to the food processor. Pulse until the mixture forms fine balls (like couscous), then transfer to a work surface. Knead to form a ball, then wrap in clingfilm and chill for 1 hour.

Cut the dough into 3 pieces and wrap each one in clingfilm. Set the pasta machine to the widest setting. Working with one piece of dough at a time, roll out once, then fold it into 3 layers. Repeat 4 times, no matter how crumbly, in order to achieve a pliable dough.

Gradually narrow the settings, rolling twice through each setting, then put it through the narrowest setting 3 times. Cover the sheet of dough with clingfilm, then fold into 3, so it is interleaved with clingfilm. Make sure it is well sealed with clingfilm to stop it drying out. When all the dough has been rolled out, cut one sheet crossways into 7-cm wide strips and cover with clingfilm.

Take one strip of pasta and put a herb leaf at one end. Fold over the other end to cover the leaf evenly. Roll twice through the machine on the second narrowest setting to stretch the leaf trapped in the pasta sandwich. Trim any rough sides, but any odd shapes are fine. Repeat with the remaining dough.

Bring a large saucepan of water to the boil, add 2 teaspoons of salt and cook the pasta in 2 batches for 1 minute each. Add half the spinach with each batch, just before draining, and drain immediately so the spinach is just wilted. Transfer to warmed pasta bowls and sprinkle with the chilli salt mixture and a few marigold petals, if available. Trail the green herb oil over the top and serve immediately.

- saffron
- purple basil (left)

purple basil ravioli
with truffle butter

a large pinch of saffron threads
2 large eggs
200 g Italian 00 pasta flour
500 g purple-fleshed potatoes, such as Blue Congo
50 g Manchego cheese, finely grated
8 sprigs of purple basil
1 egg white
sea salt
truffle oil, to serve

truffle butter

50 g jar black truffles, one thinly sliced and the rest chopped
60 g unsalted butter, cut into pieces

a pasta machine

5-cm fluted ravioli cutter

serves 4–6, makes 36 ravioli

The purple basil adds a hint of minty spice to these ravioli. The variety with a ruffled leaf (*Ocimum basilicum* 'Purple Ruffles') has an interesting liquorice flavour, but is harder to find. The ravioli can be made in advance, then cooked from frozen, which stops them sticking together.

To make the pasta dough, use a mortar and pestle to grind the saffron to a fine powder with a little salt. Add the eggs one at a time and mix thoroughly. Put the flour in a food processor and pulse for a second, then add the egg mixture. Pulse until the mixture forms fine balls (like couscous), then transfer to a work surface. Knead to form a ball, then wrap in clingfilm and chill for 1 hour.

Meanwhile, put the potatoes in a saucepan and cover with cold water. Bring to the boil, add salt and cook until very soft. Drain and, when cool enough to handle, peel off the skins. Mash and let cool, then stir in the Manchego. Pull the leaves off the sprigs of basil, chop and add to the potato mixture.

Cut the pasta dough into 3 pieces and wrap each one in clingfilm. Set the pasta machine to the widest setting. Working with one piece of dough at a time, roll out once, then fold into 3 layers. Repeat 4 times, no matter how crumbly, to achieve a pliable dough. Gradually narrow the settings, rolling twice through each setting, then put through the narrowest setting 3 times until you have a long thin sheet. Cover with clingfilm, then fold into 3, so it is interleaved with clingfilm. Make sure it is well sealed with clingfilm to stop it drying out. When all the dough has been rolled out, cut each sheet into 12 strips, 7 cm wide. Cover with clingfilm.

Put 1 teaspoon of potato mixture on one end of a strip of dough and brush egg white around it. Fold the strip over and seal, expelling any air. Stamp out with the ravioli cutter. Use extra flour if the dough is too soft. Cook in a large saucepan of lightly salted boiling water for 2–3 minutes. Drain, reserving 150 ml cooking water.

To make the truffle butter, blend the chopped truffles in a food processor with the butter and reserved cooking water. Pour over the pasta, toss gently, then serve topped with the sliced truffle and a few drops of truffle oil.

- borage
- flat leaf parsley
- lemon geranium

fresh herb risotto

800 ml light vegetable stock
100 g unsalted butter
2 tablespoons extra virgin olive oil
2 red onions, finely chopped
300 g risotto rice, such as arborio
100 ml white wine
a handful of borage leaves
350 g yellow courgettes, cut into 1-cm cubes
250 g fine or wild asparagus
a handful of flat leaf parsley leaves, coarsely chopped
a few lemon geranium leaves (optional)
100 g wild rocket
sea salt and freshly ground black pepper

to serve

80 g fresh Parmesan cheese shavings
a few borage flowers (optional)

serves 4–6

This risotto has a lovely summer quality with the yellow courgettes. Lemon geranium leaves go into it to give a citrus tang and borage leaves to give a cucumber flavour. Borage makes a wonderful alternative to spinach, particularly the young leaves. The only variety to eat (leaves and flowers) is *Borago officinalis*. Take care when picking it as the leaves are a bit furry and can produce a rash; wear gloves if you're sensitive. It gave Roman soldiers courage, although it's hard to imagine a tough legionary chewing on a blue star-shaped flower.

Put the stock in a saucepan, bring to the boil, then keep warm over very low heat.

Put half the butter and all the olive oil in a heavy-based frying pan and heat until the butter melts. Add the onions and cook until translucent but not coloured.

Stir in the rice and turn to coat in the hot oil. Increase the heat and add the wine, which will splutter and eventually be absorbed. Add half the borage leaves, then stir in 1 ladle of hot stock.

Add the courgettes and asparagus. Add 1 tablespoon of the parsley and the lemon geranium leaves, if using, then another ladle of stock. Keep adding the stock as it is absorbed.

When the rice is cooked, but still *al dente* (tender but still firm), add the remaining borage leaves and butter, and parsley, rocket and salt and pepper to taste. Remove and discard the lemon geranium leaves.

Serve topped with Parmesan shavings and borage flowers, if available.

Note Borage can be replaced with a 4-cm piece of cucumber, and lemon geranium can be replaced with the finely peeled zest of 1 lemon. Remove both before serving.

- curry leaves (left)
- garlic
- chilli
- coriander

rice and lentils with herbs

bhooni kitcheri

250 g whole red lentils (masoor dhaal)
250 g basmati rice
80 g unsalted butter
12 curry leaves or 3 bay leaves
2 cm fresh ginger, peeled and grated
2 garlic cloves, crushed
½ teaspoon chilli powder
sunflower oil, for frying
10 banana shallots or regular shallots, about 400 g, thinly sliced
a large bunch of coriander, coarsely chopped
3 fresh green chillies, deseeded and finely chopped
sea salt and freshly ground black pepper

to serve

4 hard-boiled eggs, quartered
2 lemons, cut into wedges

a heat diffuser

serves 6

The Indian kitcheri, meaning 'a bit of a mess' or a porridge, was the precursor to the British colonial dish of kedgeree. The *bhooni* part of the title means the porridge is dry not wet. Fragrant curry leaves are sold in Indian stores, but if unavailable, use bay leaves or a kaffir lime leaf. If you want to give this wonderful dish a flavour of the Raj, add poached smoked haddock before serving. Any whole lentils can be used, but beware of Puy lentils, which will turn the rice a grey colour. Whole red lentils from Indian stores taste good, but Italian brown lentils are excellent, too.

Put the lentils in a bowl, cover with water and let soak for 30 minutes. Put the rice in a sieve or colander and wash under cold running water until the water runs clear. Drain the lentils and rice.

Put the butter in a large saucepan and heat until melted. Add the drained lentils and rice and stir to coat with butter. Add 4 of the curry leaves or all the bay leaves, the ginger, garlic, chilli powder, salt and pepper. Cover with 850 ml water, stir and bring to the boil. As soon as it boils, cover with a lid and lower the heat to low (use a heat diffuser). Cook for 30 minutes.

Meanwhile, heat the oil in a frying pan, add the remaining curry leaves, if using, and fry for 10 seconds. Remove and drain on kitchen paper – the leaves crisp as they cool. Add the shallots in 2 batches and fry until crisp and golden. As they are ready, remove and drain on kitchen paper.

When the kitcheri is ready, fluff it up with a fork and fold through the coriander and two-thirds of the fried shallots and all the chopped chillies.

To serve, fluff up the rice with a fork and top with the fried curry leaves, if using, the remaining fried shallots, hard-boiled eggs and lemon wedges.

• epazote

burritos with black beans and avocado salsa

3 garlic cloves

200 g dried black beans, soaked overnight and drained

2 chipotle chillies

2 tablespoons corn or olive oil

1½ teaspoons cumin seeds

2 sprigs of epazote or winter savoury (optional)

1 onion, finely chopped

2–4 spring onions, chopped

a handful of coriander, chopped

sea salt and freshly ground black pepper

avocado and red onion salsa

1 Hass avocado

freshly squeezed juice of 1 lime

1 large red onion, chopped

10 cherry tomatoes, quartered

½ teaspoon sugar

4 tablespoons chopped fresh coriander

corn tortillas*

250 g masa harina (specially treated Mexican cornmeal)

a pinch of salt

1 tablespoon olive oil

to serve

a handful of shredded lettuce

crème fraîche or Greek yoghurt

serves 6 as a starter or 3 as a main course

**see note on dough and batter, page 4*

We have Mexico to thank for the innumerable varieties of chilli, from the fresh green fiery serrano to the fruity mahogany-coloured dried ancho. This recipe calls for smoky chipotle chilli, in a cuisine that features herbs like epazote and coriander more than spices. If you can't find masa harina, buy flour tortillas and follow the packet instructions.

Put 2 of the garlic cloves and the beans into a saucepan, add enough water to cover the beans by 3 cm, bring to the boil, reduce the heat, cover and cook for 1½–2 hours or until the beans are very tender (cooking time depends on the age of the beans). Drain the beans, reserving the cooking liquid.

Crush the remaining garlic and chop one of the chillies. Heat the oil in a large saucepan and add the whole and chopped chillies, cumin seeds and epazote, if using. Fry for 20 seconds, then add the onion. Fry for about 5 minutes, then add the crushed garlic. Cook for a further 3–4 minutes or until the onion is soft. Add the drained beans, together with a little of their cooking liquid to keep them moist. Continue to cook, stirring frequently. Add the salt and pepper and mash well, adding enough liquid to make a chunky paste, then cover.

To make the avocado and red onion salsa, scoop out the avocado flesh and cut into smallish chunks. Put it into a bowl with the lime juice, tossing well so the avocado doesn't discolour. Add the red onion, cherry tomatoes and avocado, then stir in the sugar and coriander. Mix well, cover and set aside.

To make the tortillas, put the masa harina, salt and olive oil into a mixing bowl. Gradually stir in about 325 ml water – enough to bind the mixture together into a dough. Knead briefly, shape into a ball, cover and set aside for several minutes.

Knead the dough again and divide into 6 balls, keeping them covered while working. Flatten one and roll out between 2 sheets of clingfilm. Heat a non-stick frying pan until hot. Put the tortilla into the pan and cook for 45 seconds, until the edges begin to dry out. Turn and cook for about 30 seconds more. Turn again and cook for 10 seconds. Remove and keep the tortilla warm in a tea towel or aluminium foil while you cook the remainder.

Gently reheat the beans, add the spring onions and coriander and stir gently. Put a small portion of the beans onto each tortilla and carefully roll into a burrito (a long filled and rolled tortilla). Put a little salsa onto each plate. Let guests help themselves to the shredded lettuce and crème fraîche.

- cardamom
- saffron

perfumed persian pulow

¼ teaspoon ground cinnamon

¼ teaspoon ground cardamom (preferably white, made only from the seeds, not the pods)

½ teaspoon sugar

50 g raisins, soaked in warm water for 5 minutes

25 g flaked almonds, toasted in a dry frying pan

25 g shelled unsalted pistachio nuts, coarsely chopped

100 g frozen peas, thawed and blanched in boiling water

350 g basmati rice

3 tablespoons olive oil

1 tablespoon freshly grated orange zest

a large pinch of saffron threads, soaked in 2 tablespoons hot water and 2 tablespoons orange flower water

2 tablespoons clarified butter (ghee), to serve

sea salt

serves 4–6

Iranians are undoubtedly the greatest rice cooks. Their sophisticated cuisine dates back to the ancient Persian Empire, which wooed its conquered lands with delicious food. Use only basmati for this dish, or it will disappoint, and follow the timings exactly as they work well.

Mix the cinnamon, cardamom and sugar in a small bowl and set aside. Mix the raisins, almonds, pistachios and peas in a second bowl and set aside.

Put the rice into a sieve and rinse under cold running water until the water runs clear. Transfer to a large bowl, cover with fresh cold water and soak for 2 hours. Drain well (never press the rice to drain as this damages the grains). Put about 1.25 litres water into a large saucepan, bring to the boil, add a pinch of salt, then the rice. Return to the boil and cook for 3–4 minutes without stirring. Drain well and rinse briefly in warm water.

Heat the olive oil in the same saucepan, then reduce the heat to the lowest possible. Add layers of ingredients in the following order (you will have 3–4 layers, depending on the size of the saucepan) – rice; raisins, nut and pea mixture; followed by a pinch of zest and a pinch of the spice and sugar mixture. Repeat until all the ingredients have been used, finishing with a layer of rice.

Sprinkle with the saffron and its soaking liquid. Using the end of a wooden spoon, poke a few holes in the rice all the way down to the bottom of the pan. Cover tightly with a lid lined with a tea towel, so that no steam escapes. (This step is very important – gather the edges of the towel and fold over the top of the lid to keep it from coming into contact with the flame.) Cook over very low heat for about 20 minutes (or leave it on super-low for even longer, as Iranian cooks do).

When ready to serve, remove from the heat, lift the lid and towel, pour the clarified butter over the pulow and fluff up with a fork. Serve hot with other dishes. (A delicious crust will have formed on the bottom of the pan – this is known as *tahdeeg* in Iran and it is the most coveted part of the rice!)

Note It is not usually necessary to wash and soak rice with modern methods of rice production, and you lose some of the nutritional value of the rice when doing so. However, for special and traditional dishes, such as this one, which are prepared on rare occasions, this method is well worth the effort. The results are sublime, and the soaked rice cooks in a very short time. This method is also useful when using brown basmati as it softens the texture of the unrefined grains.

- dill
- baath masala spice mix

dill baath

350 g basmati rice
6 tablespoons sunflower oil
4 tablespoons Baath Masala (page 176)

tarka

3 tablespoons sunflower oil or ghee*
1 tablespoon black mustard seeds
1 teaspoon channa dhaal (yellow lentils)
1 teaspoon urid dhaal (white lentils)
1 teaspoon cumin seeds
¾ teaspoon asafoetida (hing)
½ teaspoon ground turmeric
125 g fresh dill, central and any tough stems discarded, fronds chopped
3 tablespoons Baath Masala (page 176)
sea salt

serves 4–6

Some people are surprised that dill is used in Indian recipes, but it is relished by various communities. This South Indian recipe hails from Karnataka. In South India, where rice is king, baath (spiced rice dishes) accompany plain white rice and other dishes. They can also be eaten on their own. Make the baath masala ahead of time. You can use this for other South Indian spiced rice dishes, adding vegetables like green peppers instead of the dill, or a mixture of vegetables like carrots, peas and green beans. The spicing is quite distinctive, combining a highly fragrant toasted and ground mixture with typically Southern whole spices fried in oil (the tarka).

Put the rice into a wide, heavy saucepan with a tight-fitting lid. Add 825 ml water and bring to the boil. Reduce the heat to the lowest setting. Line the inside of the lid with a tea towel and cover tightly so that no steam escapes. (This step is very important – gather the edges of the towel and fold over the top of the lid to keep the towel from coming into contact with the flame.) Gently simmer for 15 minutes, then turn off the heat completely and let steam, still tightly covered, for a further 10 minutes. Do not be tempted to uncover the rice at any time during the cooking/steaming period.

To make the tarka, put the oil or ghee into a small saucepan and heat until hot. Add the mustard seeds, yellow and white lentils, cumin seeds, asafoetida and turmeric all at once. Cover the pan, reduce the heat to medium and let the spices sizzle and pop. Remove the pan from the heat and add the dill, baath masala and salt. Stir over low heat until the dill is wilted and the masala is well mixed – add a little water if necessary. Remove from the heat.

Transfer the freshly cooked rice to a large mixing bowl, fluff up with a fork and sprinkle the oil over the top. Add the baath masala and mix well. Stir in the tarka mixture so the rice is well coated – use two wooden forks or your hands to make sure the herbs and masala coat all the rice. Serve warm.

***Note** The choice of oil varies according to the dish, the community or the region. Maharashtrans often use groundnut oil, in Kerala, cooks rely on coconut oil and Bengalis like mustard oil, especially for fish. Karnatakans like sunflower oil or ghee.

• rosemary

pissaladière

Pissaladière is the Provençal version of pizza. Cooking the onion in white wine and olive oil adds extra sweetness. The tastes are intense, so they need a challenging sister flavour, like the highly aromatic, pine-like qualities of rosemary. The red pepper adds a hint of colour.

275 g plain flour

2 teaspoons easy-blend dried yeast

½ teaspoon salt

1 egg, beaten

1 tablespoon extra virgin olive oil

topping

1 kg white onions, thinly sliced

2 tablespoons brown caster sugar

125 ml extra virgin olive oil

150 ml white wine

1 sprig of rosemary and 2 tablespoons chopped rosemary leaves

1 large ramiro pepper

2 teaspoons anchovy paste

100 g canned anchovies, drained and halved lengthways

about 20 black olives

freshly ground black pepper

a baking sheet, about 30 x 25 cm

serves 6–8

To make the dough, put the flour, yeast and salt in a large bowl and mix briefly. Put the egg and olive oil in a small bowl, add 150 ml hand-hot water and whisk well. Make a hollow in the flour and pour in the egg mixture. Using your hand, mix until the dough comes together into a ball. Transfer to a floured work surface and knead for about 5 minutes until soft and elastic. Transfer the dough to an oiled bowl, cover with clingfilm and let rise in a warm place for 1 hour.

To make the topping, put the onions in a large, heavy-based saucepan. Stir in the sugar, 60 ml of the olive oil, the wine and the sprig of rosemary. Cook over low heat for 30 minutes, turning every 10 minutes so the onions don't burn. The liquid should evaporate leaving the onions soft and deliciously perfumed.

Using a toasting fork or tongs, hold the red pepper over a gas flame and char until blackened all over. Put in a plastic bag and let steam for 10 minutes to soften. Rub off the skin under cold, running water, then remove the seeds and slice the flesh into thin lengths. Set aside.

Transfer the dough to a floured work surface and knead for 1 minute. Roll out to a rough rectangle, then put into the baking sheet, pushing the dough to the edges and fitting it into the corners. Mix the anchovy paste with 2 tablespoons of the oil and smooth onto the dough base. Brush the edges with more oil. Remove the sprig of rosemary from the onions and stir in the chopped rosemary. Pour the mixture over the dough. Arrange the anchovies and pepper strips side by side in a diamond pattern and leave for 10 minutes at room temperature. Bake in a preheated oven at 190°C (375°F) Gas 5 for about 20 minutes. Remove from the oven, put the olives in the centre of each diamond, pour over the remaining oil, sprinkle with black pepper and return to the oven for a further 5 minutes (cover with aluminium foil if over-browning). Serve warm or at room temperature.

• sage

sage schiacciata bread

with cheese and onion

350 g unbleached bread flour

½ teaspoon sea salt, plus extra to serve

1 sachet (1 tablespoon) easy-blend dried yeast

2 tablespoons olive oil, plus extra to serve

4 large sage leaves, coarsely chopped

3 tablespoons olive oil, plus extra to serve

cheese and onion topping

30 g Manchego cheese, grated

1 red onion or 4 pink Thai shallots, sliced into rings

8 sage leaves, chopped

freshly ground black pepper

a baking sheet, dusted with flour

serves 6–8

The Italian word *schiacciata* means 'flattened', which is how this focaccia-style bread gets its name. This version is flavoured with sage, which has always been seen as a healthy herb, famous for its antiseptic qualities. It can have a very strong, medicinal flavour, so it should be used sparingly.

Put the flour, salt and yeast in a large bowl and mix well. Put the olive oil in a measuring jug, add 250 ml hand-hot water and stir well. Make a hollow in the flour and pour in the liquid. Mix with your hand and, when it all comes together, transfer to a floured work surface. Knead for 5 minutes until the dough is elastic. Put the dough in an oiled bowl, cover and let rise in a warm place for 1 hour.

Transfer the dough to a work surface, add the sage and knead for 2–3 minutes. Put the dough on the prepared baking sheet and shape it into a flat circle about 22 cm diameter, then make indentations over the surface of the dough with your fingers. Brush with the olive oil and leave at room temperature for 10 minutes.

Cook in a preheated oven at 200°C (400°F) Gas 6 for 10 minutes. Remove from the oven, spread the grated cheese on top, followed by the onion rings, black pepper and sage leaves. Cook for a further 10 minutes, then increase the heat to 220°C (425°F) Gas 7 and cook for another 5 minutes or until cooked. To test, insert a skewer in the middle. It should come out clean – if it doesn't, cook for 5 minutes longer.

Sprinkle with sea salt flakes and more olive oil, then serve.

sweet things

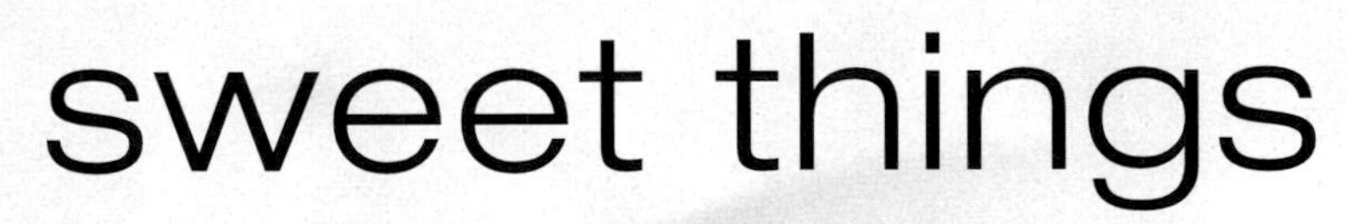

• kaffir lime leaves

summer fruit salad
with kaffir lime sorbet

40 g kaffir lime leaves

225 g caster sugar

150 ml white wine, such as pinot grigio

1 egg white

1 orange-fleshed melon, such as Charentais or cantaloupe, halved and deseeded

1 green-fleshed melon, such as honeydew, halved and deseeded

1 small watermelon, preferably seedless, halved

2 ripe mangoes, cheeks removed

4 large kiwi fruit, peeled

1 dragon fruit, peeled (optional)*

an ice cream maker (optional)

melon ballers

serves 4–6

Use any fruit that you can scoop out with a melon baller for this salad. Kaffir lime leaf, with its clean citrus flavours, is used to perfume the syrup. Pour the syrup over the fruit and churn the remainder into a soft sorbet. It seems like a lot of leaves, but it works. Buy the lime leaves in big bags from Chinese or Asian markets, then use them fresh or freeze and use straight from frozen. Any leftovers can be used to make Thai curries. The leaves grow in pairs, as shown.

Tear the kaffir lime leaves and arrange in layers in a saucepan, sprinkling the sugar between the layers. Set aside for several hours or overnight to develop the flavours. Add 250 ml water and slowly heat to dissolve the sugar. Boil for 1 minute, then transfer to a bowl to chill.

Strain the syrup and measure 200 ml into a bowl. Add the wine and 100 ml water, then chill in the refrigerator. Set the remainder aside until you are ready to make the salad.

Add the egg white to the chilled syrup and wine and whisk just to break it up. Transfer to an ice cream maker and churn according to the manufacturer's instructions. Eat immediately or store in the freezer. Alternatively, put the mixture into a large freezer-proof container and freeze, stirring occasionally to break up the ice crystals.

When ready to serve, scoop balls of melon, mango, kiwi fruit and dragon fruit into a bowl using one or several sizes of melon ballers. Pour the reserved syrup over the top and keep cool until needed. Serve with scoops of kaffir lime sorbet.

***Note** Dragon fruit is a large pink tropical fruit covered with green and yellow horns. Its flesh is sweet, with tiny black seeds like vanilla. It is sold in Chinese and Asian markets, and sometimes in up-market greengrocers and supermarkets. If unavailable, omit or use another tropical fruit, such as papaya.

• ginger
• lemongrass (left)

lemongrass-ginger syrup

with dragon's eyes

250 g caster sugar

2 cm fresh ginger, peeled and thinly sliced

3 stalks of lemongrass, bruised and coarsely chopped

2 starfruit (carambola)

36 fresh longans or lychees, peeled and deseeded, or 2 cans, about 560 g each, drained

finely grated zest and juice of 1 unwaxed lime

2 baking sheets, lined with silicone baking parchment

serves 6

'Dragon's eyes' is the romantic name for the longan fruit, a relative of the lychee (which you can use as an alternative) – either fresh or canned. Longans, which look like huge bunches of brown hairy grapes, are only available fresh in autumn, and you'll see special vendors selling them in Asian markets. Lemongrass and ginger are the distinctive flavours of Thailand. They make an easy syrup for this simple pudding to finish a Thai-style dinner and, like other Asian ingredients, are easy to use from frozen.

Put the sugar and 350 ml water in a heavy-based saucepan and heat gently to dissolve. Increase the heat, add the ginger and lemongrass and boil for 8 minutes until syrupy but still pale. Remove the pan from the heat and let cool completely.

To make the starfruit crisps, peel off the brown ridges of the starfruit with a vegetable peeler. Slice the fruit crossways very thinly using a mandoline. Arrange on kitchen paper and brush the top side with a little of the cold syrup and set them on the prepared baking sheets, painted side down. Lightly brush the top side with syrup. Transfer to a preheated oven and cook at 110°C (225°F) Gas ¼. Gently turn them over after 30 minutes, return to the oven and dry them out for a further 15 minutes. Carefully peel off the baking parchment.

Strain the syrup, leaving in a few bits of ginger. Add the longans, lime juice and zest to the syrup and chill until ready to serve with the starfruit crisps.

Note To test if the starfruit crisps are ready, take one out – it should crisp as it cools. They can be kept stored in an airtight container until ready to use. Apples can be cooked in the same way (there's no need to core or peel them).

• violets (left)
• tansy

tansy panna cotta

a medium bunch of fresh young tansy leaves, sweet cicely or 6 bay leaves

600 ml double cream

40 g caster sugar

75 g white chocolate drops

3 sheets leaf gelatine or 1 sachet powdered gelatine

crystallized flowers (optional)

1 egg white

a large handful of violas (heartsease) or sweet violets

caster sugar, for sprinkling

six 100-ml ramekins or moulds

a heat diffuser

serves 6

Tansy is an old-fashioned herb, which is available in most garden centres, and is very useful in the garden as a pest controller. A perennial, it grows to a fine height and has bright yellow, button-like flowers, and was used in Victorian nosegays. If unavailable, use sweet cicely or flavour the cream with bay leaves.

To crystallize the flowers, put the egg white in a bowl and whisk lightly to break it up. Paint the violets lightly with the egg white, then put the caster sugar in a tea strainer and sprinkle it all over the flowers. Transfer to parchment paper and leave in a warm, dry place until crisp. They will keep in an airtight container for about 1 week.

To prepare the panna cotta, strip the fern-like young tansy leaves from the centre stem or the sweet cicely leaves in the same way. Purée in a blender with 60 ml of water and 60 ml of the double cream. Pour through a nylon sieve set over a bowl and press out the juice with a ladle and reserve, discarding the pulp.

Pour the remaining cream into a saucepan and heat gently over low heat to just below boiling point (use a heat diffuser so it takes about 15 minutes). Add the sugar and chocolate drops and mix to dissolve. Soften the gelatine in cold water for 10 minutes and add to the pan and stir to dissolve. Cool for 20 minutes. Add the tansy juice and stir well.

Arrange the ramekins on a tray, pour in the mixture, then cover and chill to set. To serve, unmould the panna cottas by dipping the bases in hot water, then invert onto a plate. Top with the crystallized flowers, if using.

• rose geranium

rose meringuettes
with rose geranium syrup

12 rose geranium leaves

160 g caster sugar

1 teaspoon red cake sugar crystals (from the baking section of the supermarket or specialist suppliers)

2 large egg whites

a pinch of cream of tartar

crystallized leaves and petals

petals from 4 small rosebuds

a handful of rose geranium flowers

small leaves from the top of rose geranium sprigs

1 egg white

caster sugar, for sprinking

chantilly cream

300 ml double cream

2 teaspoons sifted icing sugar

1 teaspoon rosewater

2 baking sheets, lined with baking parchment

makes 12

These meringues have rose-scented sugar as their base. Scented geraniums are available in garden centres – ask for *Pelargonium* 'Graveolens' (rose geranium), *Pelargonium capitatum* (wild rose geranium) or the variety 'Attar of Roses'. It is the leaves, rather than the flowers, which have the strongest scent. For the best scent, let the sugar sit with the leaves for 4 days. Alternatively, use a few extra drops of rosewater in the mixture or strongly scented unsprayed rose petals.

To crystallize the leaves and petals, follow the method on page 147.

To scent the sugar, put the geranium leaves and sugar in an airtight jar and set aside for 4 days. When ready to make the meringues, remove the leaves from the sugar and discard. Put 60 g of the scented sugar into a clean electric coffee grinder, add the red cake sugar crystals and grind to a fine powder.

Put the egg whites and cream of tartar in a bowl and whisk until firm peaks form. Whisk in the remaining 100 g scented caster sugar, a spoonful at a time. Gently fold in the pink sugar powder a little at a time.

Spoon 12 piles, about 1 heaped tablespoon each and 5 cm in diameter, onto the prepared baking sheets. Cook in a preheated oven at 110°C (225°F) Gas ¼ for about 1 hour (open the oven door a little if bubbles appear) until firm. Remove from the oven and let cool for 5 minutes, then peel off the baking parchment. Put them back on the parchment to cool completely. Store in an airtight container until needed.

To make the chantilly cream, put the cream, icing sugar and rosewater in a bowl and beat until soft peaks form. Use the cream to sandwich the meringues together, then serve sprinkled with crystallized leaves and petals.

fig on a cushion
with thyme-scented syrup

500 g puff pastry

6 sprigs of thyme, with flowers if available

75 g caster sugar

2 teaspoons grenadine (pomegranate syrup)

150–200 g triple-crème cheese, such as Saint André, cut horizontally to make 4 discs

6 fresh ripe figs, preferably black (purple), halved vertically

1 egg yolk, beaten with 2 teaspoons water

2 pastry cutters or templates, about 14 cm and 11 cm diameter

serves 4

This irresistible recipe is dessert and cheese rolled into one and the fig and thyme complement each other perfectly. It features a broad-leaved thyme, the creeping *Thymus pulegioides*, which is in leaf all year round, with beautiful mauve flowers in summer. Orange-scented thyme, *Thymus* 'Fragrantissimus', would provide another interesting flavour.

Put the pastry on a floured surface and roll out to about 28 cm square. Using the 14-cm pastry cutter or template, cut out 4 circles. Use the edge of the knife to 'knock up' or separate the layers of pastry so they will rise well. Set the circles on a baking sheet and chill for 30 minutes.

Strip the leaves off 4 sprigs of thyme and put them in a small saucepan. Add the sugar and 75 ml water. Set over medium heat and slowly dissolve the sugar. Boil for 4 minutes. Remove from the heat, add the grenadine, let cool, then chill.

Make slashes at 1-cm intervals around the edges of the pastry circles and score an inner circle to join up the slashes, or use the 11-cm pastry cutter, but don't cut all the way through. Prick the inside of the inner circle with a fork.

Put 1 round of cheese in the middle of each pastry. Strip the leaves off the remaining 2 sprigs of thyme and sprinkle on top of the cheese. Arrange 3 fig halves on each piece of cheese.

Brush around the edges of the pastry with the beaten egg yolk, but don't let it drip down the sides or the tarts won't rise. Chill until ready to cook. Bake in a preheated oven at 220°C (425°F) Gas 7 for 20–25 minutes until puffed and golden. Strain the scented syrup, pour it over the figs, add a few pink thyme flowers, if using, then serve.

- cinnamon
- lemon balm

moroccan melissa pastries

200 g shelled pistachios
200 g ground almonds
50 g icing sugar
75 g caster sugar
½ teaspoon ground cinnamon, plus extra to decorate
2 teaspoons rosewater or orange flower water
a handful of lemon balm or lemon verbena, finely chopped
150 g unsalted butter, at room temperature
8 large sheets of filo pastry
sifted icing sugar, to decorate

a baking sheet

makes 8

These crumbly Moroccan pastries are usually flavoured with mint and finely grated lemon zest. This version can be made with two close relations of mint – lemon balm or fragrant lemon verbena. Lemon balm is also known by its pretty name, melissa, from the Greek word for honey bee. It smells marvellous and also makes a cool, invigorating drink at the height of summer.

Put the pistachios in a clean coffee grinder and grind to a fine powder. Reserve 2 tablespoons of the pistachio powder and put the remainder in a bowl, then add the ground almonds, icing sugar, caster sugar, cinnamon, rosewater and lemon balm.

Add 100 g of the butter to the nut mixture and mash together to form a paste. Chill for 10 minutes, then divide into 8 portions.

Melt the remaining butter in a small saucepan. Arrange 1 sheet of filo on a work surface with the long edge towards you (keep the rest covered so it doesn't dry out). Brush the edges of the sheet with melted butter and spread one portion of the paste in a line on the front edge of the filo – leave it loose with a few gaps, so it doesn't split when turned in a spiral. Roll it up, away from you to make a thin log, then brush with a little more butter to make it pliable. Coil the log into a spiral and tuck the end underneath to seal. Brush with extra butter and put on a baking sheet. Repeat to make 8 spirals in total.

Bake in a preheated fan oven at 200°C (400°F) Gas 6 for 20–25 minutes until crisp and golden brown. (If using a regular oven, adjust the cooking time and temperature according to the manufacturer's instructions.)

Remove from the oven and let cool on a wire rack. Dust with icing sugar, then sprinkle the reserved ground pistachio powder and cinnamon over the top in wiggly lines.

- nutmeg
- cinnamon

sweet potato and banana spiced fritters

2 large sweet potatoes
2 plantains or under-ripe bananas
oil, for deep-frying

frothy batter*

275 g plain flour
½ teaspoon freshly grated nutmeg
2 teaspoons ground cinnamon
about 425 ml sparkling water

to serve

brown sugar or icing sugar
sweet salsa or chutney, such as Plum Chutney (page 167; optional)

serves 6–8: makes about 38 fritters

**see note on dough and batter, page 4*

This is a Caribbean recipe with its African roots in evidence. Sweet potatoes are great fritter vegetables, melting in your mouth with creamy sweetness. If you can find true plantains (platanos) at a shop selling exotic fruit and vegetables, snap them up – they, too, are perfect fritter material. Otherwise, under-ripe bananas will be convenient substitutes for plantains. Nutmeg (and its outer cover of mace) was originally to be found only in the Spice Islands of Indonesia, but is now one of the major crops of Grenada in the Caribbean.

To make the batter, put the flour, nutmeg and cinnamon into a large bowl and stir well. Make a well in the centre and gradually whisk in enough sparkling water to make a smooth batter, thick enough to coat the back of a spoon. Cover with a tea towel and set aside for 20 minutes.

Cut the sweet potatoes into 1.5-cm slices, then cut in half (you should have about 28 half-moon pieces). Cut the plantains into 2.5-cm slices (about 10), because they will cook much faster.

Fill a deep saucepan one-third full of oil and heat to 190°C (375°F) or until a cube of bread browns in 30 seconds. Working in batches and using tongs, dip a piece of plantain or banana into the batter, coat well, then slide it into the hot oil – do not overcrowd the pan. Fry until golden brown all over. Remove with a slotted spoon, drain in a colander lined with kitchen paper, then transfer to a serving plate and keep them warm while you cook the sweet potatoes, again in batches.

Sprinkle with sugar and serve hot. These fritters are great on their own, but you can also serve them with sweet salsa or chutney.

vanilla poached pears

8 small pears, slightly under-ripe

1 lemon, halved

1 bottle sweet white wine (750 ml), such as Moscatel de Valencia

3–4 tablespoons golden caster sugar or vanilla sugar*

1 vanilla pod, split lengthways with a small, sharp knife

good-quality vanilla ice cream or crème fraîche, to serve

serves 4

Fruits and spices have long been deemed ideal partners; think apples and cinnamon, mango and ginger, or pickling spices for fruit chutneys. Delicately poached fruits such as plums, peaches or pears with vanilla or other 'sweet' spices are part of the French culinary repertoire. Today this combination is evident in much of Europe, a Gallic gift bestowed on the rest of the Continent, just like the classical skills and refinement of the French kitchen. Choose firm pears that will hold up well.

Using a vegetable peeler, peel the pears but leave the stem intact. Hold the pears over a bowl as you work and rub the lemon half and its juice over the fruit to prevent discoloration. To achieve a smooth surface, rub the pears with a clean tea towel and rub again with the lemon.

Put the wine into a stainless steel or enamel (non-reactive) saucepan, just big enough to hold the pears, stems upward. Add the sugar and 100 ml water and heat, stirring until the sugar dissolves. Add the split vanilla pod, pears and the remaining lemon juice. Simmer gently for about 10 minutes, until the pears are tender but still firm. Remove with a slotted spoon and transfer to a serving bowl.

Boil the poaching liquid hard and reduce by half until syrupy, about 10 minutes. (Scrape the sides of the pan while the liquid is boiling so all the vanilla flecks stay in the liquid.)

Pour the syrup and vanilla pod over the fruits. Let cool and serve at room temperature or cold, with vanilla ice cream or crème fraîche.

Variations Try combinations of other spices such as cinnamon, cloves, star anise or even black pepper.

***Note** To make vanilla sugar, put a vanilla pod or pods into a jar, cover with sugar and seal. The pods can be dried after each use and returned to the jar.

creamy saffron pudding

seviyan kheer/shavagay payasa

50 g unsalted butter

4 tablespoons raw unsalted cashew nuts

1½ tablespoons raisins

75 g Indian wheat vermicelli, broken into 3-cm lengths*

725 ml whole milk

85 g sugar

½ teaspoon ground cardamom, preferably white (made only from the seeds, not pods), or the seeds from 1–2 cardamom pods

a large pinch of saffron threads

topping

2 tablespoons unsalted butter

1 tablespoon raisins

1 tablespoon raw unsalted cashew nuts

1 tablespoon shelled unsalted pistachio nuts

a few saffron strands soaked in 1 tablespoon warm milk

a pinch of ground cardamom

serves 4–6

This scented vermicelli milk pudding is imbued with all the fragrance of saffron and cardamom (other versions include rosewater) and is delicious hot or cold. It is a favourite all over India, known as *payasa* or *payasam* in the South and *kheer* in the North. Spices vary only slightly, but can make all the difference in flavour. Cashew nuts are produced in South India and Goa. In the North, it might be made with pistachios, almonds or charoli nuts (a little like pine nuts), or a combination.

Melt the butter in a heavy saucepan. Add the cashews and raisins and fry until the cashews are golden and the raisins plump. Add the broken vermicelli and fry briefly in the butter, until it wilts and is evenly golden. (It will feel as if you are frying straw at this stage, but the vermicelli softens quickly.)

Add 500 ml of the milk and bring to the boil over medium-high heat, being careful not to let it burn. As soon as the milk reaches boiling point, lower the heat and add the sugar, cardamom and saffron and stir. Cook for a few minutes until the mixture thickens and the vermicelli is cooked through. The mixture will be quite thick at this stage – if you like a more runny consistency, add the remaining milk at this point. Stir well and remove from the heat, but keep hot.

To prepare the topping, heat the butter in a small saucepan, add the raisins, cashews and pistachios and stir-fry for a few minutes until golden, without letting the butter burn.

Stir the pudding again and spoon into small bowls. Sprinkle with the soaked saffron, ground cardamom and buttered cashews, pistachios and raisins and serve hot.

Variations You could also make this pudding with just one of the spices listed, or with saffron and rosewater. If you use commercially made rosewater, it will usually contain citric acid, so you must wait until the pudding cools completely before adding, or the milk will curdle. When ready to serve, top with a few unsprayed rose petals.

***Note** Indian wheat vermicelli is available from Indian and Pakistani shops. Alternatively, use regular vermicelli pasta.

• nutmeg (left)
• cardamom

ricotta-stuffed dates

with spicy arab coffee

100 g ricotta cheese

2 teaspoons golden caster sugar

1 teaspoon freshly grated nutmeg

18 best quality dates, such as mozafati or medjool, pitted

arab spiced coffee

4 heaped tablespoons best quality coarsely ground coffee

1½ teaspoons cardamom seeds, plus 4 whole cardamom pods, bruised

1 teaspoon rosewater or orange flower water

demerara sugar, to serve (optional)

serves 6

Arab coffee is a symbol of Arab hospitality, served black and in tiny cups, with as many refills as you can handle. It is actually considered an insult to drink only one cup! Poured from elegant, long-spouted coffee pots with an extra cardamom pod wedged in the spout, the coffee comes out in a fragrant arc. Arabs usually drink it unsweetened but you may wish to serve it with brown sugar. The indigenous date palm has long been essential throughout North Africa and the Middle East. In the arid climate and desert terrain, nomadic peoples from the Atlantic to the Persian Gulf depend on this source of nourishment. Dates are often stuffed with local cheeses, but come into their own when stuffed with sweetly spiced ricotta. Find the best dates you can, for example mozafati (known as the king of dates) or medjool. The nutmeg must be freshly grated for this recipe.

To prepare the dates, put the ricotta cheese into a small bowl and whisk well. Add the sugar and nutmeg and mix until smooth. Stuff each date with a little of the spiced ricotta and serve on a small plate.

To make the arab spiced coffee, put the ground coffee and cardamom seeds in a large saucepan, then add 1.25 litres boiling water. (If you prefer even stronger coffee, use only 950 ml). Add the rosewater and return to the boil. Reduce the heat and simmer for 1 minute, then turn off the heat. Cover with a lid and set aside for about 30 minutes.

Before serving, gently warm the coffee without boiling and transfer to a heated coffee pot. Pour into small espresso or Arab coffee cups and serve.

- vanilla
- cinnamon

mexican chocolate

with vanilla cream

125 g organic chocolate, at least 70 per cent cocoa solids, broken into pieces

1.5 litres whole milk

4 tablespoons sugar

2 teaspoons ground cinnamon

cinnamon sticks, to serve (optional)

vanilla whipped cream

250 ml whipping cream

1 vanilla pod*

serves 6

In Mexico, hot chocolate has always been known simply as 'chocolate', and it was here of course that the world's love affair with the addictively good substance began. The Aztecs, like the Olmecs before them, used the cacao bean only for the drink, making it with water, sometimes adding native vanilla and even chillies. The conquistadors altered the recipe to include sugar, cinnamon (showing the Moorish influence in Spain) and supposedly anise and pepper, the latter presumably to replace the hotter chilli. Today Mexican chocolate is a hybrid, closer to the hot cocoa we all know and love. Mexicans use real chocolate pieces made with sugar, cinnamon and almonds. This recipe uses top quality chocolate – at least 70 per cent cocoa solids and organic and fairtrade on principle – and perfumes the resulting elixir with cinnamon.

To make the vanilla whipped cream, put the cream into a bowl and whisk with an electric beater until light and fluffy, with soft peaks. Slit the vanilla pod lengthways and carefully scrape out all the seeds, then gently fold them into the cream. (The vanilla pod can be used to make vanilla sugar, page 156.)

To make the hot chocolate, put the chocolate into a heatproof bowl set over a saucepan of gently simmering water and melt – don't let the bowl touch the water or the chocolate will be spoiled. Pour the milk into a large saucepan and stir in the sugar and cinnamon. Heat until gently simmering – do not boil. Whisk a ladle of the milk into the melted chocolate then pour the mixture into the saucepan, whisking until smooth. Ladle into 6 mugs. Top each with a generous spoonful of vanilla whipped cream and serve hot with a cinnamon stick stirrer, if using.

Note Buy organic and fairtrade chocolate whenever you can. Organic brands are produced without lindane, a harmful hormone-disrupting pesticide that may soon be banned in Europe. The fairtrade mark makes a stand against the chocolate slave trade going on in the Ivory Coast and nearby. If you can, question the origins of the chocolate you are buying, make a stand and make a difference.

little extras

salsa roja

Mexican restaurants and homes everywhere keep this sauce or condiment on the table or beside the stove. Add it to anything you think needs a bit of livening up. It also makes a great accompaniment for corn chips served with cocktails, such as margaritas or bloody marys. New Mexico chillies have a smoky, earthy flavour but they aren't overly hot. You can use hotter dried chillies if you prefer – try chipotle, ancho, pasilla or cascabel.

12 dried New Mexico chillies
125 ml sunflower oil
3 garlic cloves, halved
1 tablespoon chopped fresh oregano
6 large, ripe tomatoes, skinned and deseeded
sea salt and freshly ground black pepper
corn chips, to serve

makes about 500 ml

Break the chillies in half and shake out the seeds. Heat the oil in a frying pan, add the chillies and fry until they turn bright red. Remove with a slotted spoon and put into a bowl. Cover with water and let soak for about 30 minutes.

Add the garlic to the pan and fry until golden. Transfer to a food processor, add the drained chillies and chop coarsely. Add the oregano and tomatoes and chop again. Add salt and pepper to taste and serve with corn chips.

chilito

Chilito is a crunchy relish from Mexico made with two or three chilli varieties, usually served alongside main courses, burritos or corn chips. It reveals the nuances of various chillies, and brings their individual flavours, not just their heat, to the fore. This recipe uses liquorice-like pasilla chilli flakes, smoky chipotle chillies and jalapeño slices.

¼ teaspoon pasilla chilli flakes, with seeds
1 chipotle chilli, deseeded and chopped
6 thick slices jalapeño in brine or 1 large fresh jalapeño, deseeded
about 5 large cabbage leaves, tough stalks trimmed
1 small onion
1 tablespoon chopped fresh oregano or marjoram
3 tablespoons white wine vinegar
3 tablespoons rice vinegar
5 tablespoons pineapple juice
sea salt, to taste
Burritos (page 131) or corn chips, to serve

serves 6 as a relish

Soak the dried pasilla and chipotle chillies in 2 teaspoons warm water for about 15 minutes, then drain. Finely chop the jalapeños. Set aside.

Finely shred the cabbage in a food processor and transfer to a bowl. Repeat with the onion and add to the bowl. Add the oregano, chillies and salt and toss well.

Mix the vinegars and juice in a small jug and add to the bowl. Mix well (the liquid is just enough to coat the vegetables – it is not meant to submerge them), then set aside for 1–2 hours to develop the flavours. Serve with burritos or corn chips.

plum chutney

Chutney, a cherished sweet and spicy condiment on the British table, is an Anglo-Indian remnant from the days of the East India Company and the Raj. Homemade versions, however, have always been popular in England – just another aspect of the national taste for jams and pickles to serve with bread, cheese and cold meats. They have acquired a distinctively British flavour, different from their originals in India. In fact, authentic Indian chutneys are often more akin to relishes.

800 g plums, about 14, pitted and chopped
225 g raisins
1 large onion, chopped
½ teaspoon salt
150 ml cider vinegar
1 recipe Pickling Spices (page 173), in a spice ball or tied up in muslin
½ teaspoon ground ginger
a good pinch of freshly grated nutmeg
140 g sugar or brown sugar

two 500-ml sterilized preserving jars with non-metal lids (page 4)

2 wax discs

makes 800 ml

Put the plums, raisins, onion and salt in a stainless steel preserving pan or heavy-based saucepan and add the vinegar. Stir, then add the ball or bag of pickling spices. Bring to the boil, reduce the heat and simmer gently for about 40 minutes, stirring occasionally. Be careful not to scorch the chutney as it cooks and thickens.

Add the ginger, nutmeg and sugar and mix well. Keep a close eye on the chutney and cook for another 10–15 minutes, stirring regularly to make sure it doesn't burn. It should be dark and tangy yet sweet and thick. As it cools and sets, it will become thicker still.

Remove the ball or bag of pickling spices and pour the chutney into the sterilized jars while still hot. Line the lids with wax paper and seal the jars. Tighten the lids when the chutney has cooled a little.

Note Use a stainless steel pan for making chutney, rather than copper, which will react with the vinegar. Seal the top of the chutney with wax discs and use non-metal lids (vinegar will corrode metal).

tomsatina chutney
with basil and thyme

This chutney is good to eat with strong organic farmhouse Cheddar-style cheese. If you have thyme growing in your garden, you should prune it hard in summer, just as the thyme is flowering, so that it has another growth spurt before autumn. You can use the cuttings for recipes like these. Basil should be in full flavour at the same time.

24 ripe, well-flavoured vine tomatoes, about 2.25 kg

10 banana shallots, finely chopped, about 300 g

3 tablespoons yellow mustard seeds

1 tablespoon allspice berries

2 tablespoons thyme leaves

250 g caster sugar

300 ml cider vinegar

a large bunch of basil, chopped

sea salt and freshly ground black pepper

four 450-g sterilized preserving jars (page 4)

makes 1.8 kg

Cut the tomatoes in half, cut out the cores and chop the flesh. Put in a stainless steel preserving pan or a heavy-based saucepan and add the shallots and mustard seeds. Wrap the allspice berries in muslin and add to the pan. Cook over gentle heat until the tomato juices start to run. Add the thyme, increase the heat and simmer for about 45 minutes, until reduced by about one-third.

Add the sugar and lower the heat until it dissolves. Add the vinegar, basil, salt and pepper. Increase the heat again and simmer until it thickens, about 30 minutes. Remove the muslin-wrapped allspice berries and pour the chutney into the sterilized jars while still hot.

Line the lids with wax paper and seal the jars. Tighten the lids when the chutney has cooled a little.

Note This chutney is also good with 1 tablespoon of chopped black olives folded into about 5 tablespoons of chutney before serving. Serve with a young pecorino cheese and crisp Italian *carta de musica* as a snack with drinks.

herb butters

Herb or 'compound' butters, as they are known, are handy to have in the refrigerator or freezer – just add a spoonful to fish, grilled meat, hot potatoes or other vegetables. The flavours trapped in the butter are a revelation, so experiment with different herbs. Here are some ideas to start you off. Other great combinations include: dill leaves and salted anchovy fillets; mint and fresh pomegranate juice; lovage and walnuts; and fennel leaves and rose petals.

chivry butter

a large bunch of mixed herbs, such as parsley, tarragon, chervil, salad burnet and chives, about 65 g

150 g salted butter

1½ tablespoons finely chopped shallot

makes 250 ml

Strip the leaves off the stalks and blanch in a saucepan of boiling water for 30 seconds. Tip into a colander and refresh under cold running water.

Drain the herbs, pat dry and chop coarsely. Melt 2 tablespoons of the butter in a small frying pan, add the shallot and cook over low heat until slightly softened but not browned, about 2 minutes. Let cool.

Pour into a food processor, then add the herbs and remaining butter. Pulse until smooth, then transfer to a sheet of greaseproof paper or clingfilm and roll into a log. Alternatively, spoon into little butter dishes, smooth off the tops with a knife, then chill until firm.

nasturtium and savory butter

5 sprigs of savory

8 nasturtium leaves

8 nasturtium flowers

150 g salted butter

makes 200 ml

Strip the leaves from the sprigs of savory and chop finely. Chop the nasturtium leaves and flowers, then put in a food processor with the butter and pulse to mix.

basil, pine nut and chilli butter

50 g pine nuts, lightly toasted in a dry frying pan

4 tablespoons chopped basil leaves

1 small red chilli, deseeded and finely chopped

150 g salted butter

makes 300 ml

Put the pine nuts in a small food processor, then grind as finely as possible. Add the remaining ingredients and pulse to mix. Transfer to a sheet of greaseproof paper or clingfilm and roll into a log. Alternatively, spoon into little butter dishes, smooth off the tops with a knife, then chill until firm.

herb vinegars

There are two methods for making herb-infused vinegars. Either push a sprig or two into a bottle of vinegar and replace the lid, or boil 500 ml vinegar for every 65 g of herb leaves. Pour over the leaves, set aside to infuse for 2 weeks, then strain and pour into sterilized bottles (page 4) and seal with tight-fitting corks. Herb vinegars can be used for salad dressings and also to flavour meat or fish. Try the following combinations or experiment with different herbs and vinegars.

- White wine vinegar with tarragon.
- Red wine vinegar with rosemary.
- Cider vinegar with applemint.
- Rice vinegar with Thai sweet basil.
- Champagne vinegar with rose petals or rose geranium leaves.

herb oils

Any herb can be used to flavour oil, especially if you have large quantities of a particular herb in the garden and the hot sun has strengthened the volatile oils. Some people prefer to use the best quality extra virgin olive oil, but any olive oil will do.

- The method for most woody herbs and tender leaves is simply to put a sprig or two in the bottle and leave until the flavour is to your liking.

- For soft herbs like basil, pull the leaves from a large bunch, plunge them into boiling water, drain and instantly refresh under cold running water. Dry thoroughly on kitchen paper. Put the leaves and 300 ml olive oil in a food processor or blender and blend well. Transfer the resulting purée to a bowl and leave to infuse overnight. Strain the wonderful bright green oil through a muslin-lined sieve, pour into sterilized bottles (page 4) and store in the refrigerator. It can be used straight away or within 10 days.

tisanes

A tisane is a herb tea, made with herbs (usually the leaves) or spices infused in boiling water. Different herbs or spices are often combined and flowers are sometimes included as well. For centuries, tisanes have been used all over the world to treat illnesses, soothe the nerves, wake people up, or simply because they taste good. Here are some time-honoured favourites – you can adjust the strength of the tisane according to taste.

• Tulsi tisane is made of Greek basil or holy basil, called *tulsi* in India. It is a holy plant and was Krishna's favourite. He preferred the humble tulsi leaf to any of the flowers in the garden. In India, it isn't used for any purposes other than those of a spiritual nature.

Put a handful of basil leaves and the zest of 1 unwaxed orange in a teapot, add 600 ml boiling water and leave to infuse. Serve sweetened with 2 teaspoons honey (optional).

• Hyssop tisane is said to be good for colds in the chest.

Put a handful of hyssop leaves in a teapot, add 600 ml boiling water and leave to infuse. Serve sweetened with 2 teaspoons of honey (optional).

Variations

• Ginger tea or peppermint tea will soothe an upset stomach.

• Lemon balm tea will invigorate.

• Rosemary, especially when infused with honey, not only tastes good but helps with physical and mental strain (and is better for you than a caffeine-laden cappuccino).

• Another morning reviver is lemon verbena with peppermint and rose petals.

american spice mixes

From apple pie spice and Jamaican jerk seasoning to Mexican salsas and barbecue sauce, many American mixes are most widely known in their commercial forms, despite being based on traditional blends. Many of their ingredients are in fact native to the Americas – where would spice lovers be without chillies, cayenne, Tabasco, vanilla or allspice? Other spices, such as cumin and nutmeg, were brought to the Americas by the Spaniards.

jerk seasoning paste

This typical Jamaican seasoning is spread over meat (especially pork), poultry or fish before it is grilled or baked. It includes the native spices – allspice and chillies.

3–4 habanero chillies, deseeded

1 teaspoon chopped fresh thyme

3 garlic cloves, coarsely chopped

1 bay leaf

1 teaspoon allspice berries (about 20)

¼ teaspoon freshly grated nutmeg

3 spring onions, chopped

2 plum tomatoes, skinned (fresh or canned)

freshly squeezed juice of ½ lime

80 ml groundnut oil

½ teaspoon salt

Using a food processor or a mortar and pestle, grind the ingredients to a smooth paste. Use immediately or store in the refrigerator for up to 2 days.

cajun spice blend

This tasty blend is based on the three peppers – black, white and native cayenne. Cajun spice flavours everything from blackened fish to hearty gumbo and jambalaya, and can also be used as a barbecue rub for chicken and meat.

¼ teaspoon black peppercorns

¼ teaspoon white peppercorns

½ teaspoon cumin seeds

½ teaspoon coriander seeds

½ teaspoon cayenne pepper

½ teaspoon paprika

½ teaspoon celery salt

Crush the whole spices with a mortar and pestle until coarsely ground. Add the cayenne, paprika and celery salt and mix well. Store in an airtight container.

european spice mixes

It was perhaps because Europe's native spices were few in number (dill, fennel, caraway and coriander seeds, and juniper berries) that it became such a market for everyone else's. In the past, spices that are difficult to come by today, such as cubeb, grains of paradise, long pepper and galangal, were more readily available. Early spice blends from France and Italy often incorporated such spice gems.

pickling spices

This spice combination is typical of those used in Britain to make pickles and chutneys. Other spices, such as chillies, mace and occasionally dill seeds, could also be included.

1½ teaspoons coriander seeds

1 teaspoon allspice berries

½ teaspoon whole cloves (about 10)

¼ teaspoon black peppercorns

¾ teaspoon mustard seeds (yellow or brown)

Tie the spices in a muslin bag or put in a meshed spice ball. Suspend in the pickle or chutney while it is cooking or, if spicing vinegar, put directly into the vinegar and leave to infuse before straining and using.

quatre épices

The name of this French blend means 'four spices'. It usually contains the spices in this recipe, but it can also include ginger or allspice. It is used to flavour soups, stews, vegetables and the famous spiced bread, pain d'épices.

½ teaspoon whole cloves (about 10)

1 cinnamon stick

¼ teaspoon black peppercorns

1 teaspoon freshly grated nutmeg

Grind the whole spices to a fine powder, then mix in the grated nutmeg. Store in an airtight container.

mixed spice

For those who think of English food as plain, it is interesting to note that the English have used spices to varying degrees for at least 1,500 years, in both sweet and savoury dishes. Mixed spice is used in cakes, breads and puddings and is similar to American apple pie spice and pumpkin pie spice. Nutmeg and mace, both from the same tree, are essentials in this mixture.

¼ cinnamon stick

1 teaspoon whole cloves (about 20)

2 blades of mace, or 1 teaspoon ground mace

¾ teaspoon freshly grated nutmeg

Grind the spices together to a fine powder and store in an airtight container. A common variation is to add a few allspice berries to the mixture.

spice mixes of africa and the middle east

The use of spices in this region dates back to the world's earliest written records and cultures. The camel caravans, more than 3,000 years ago, introduced the western world to the pleasure of spices, and even today the spice bazaars of Cairo, Morocco and Istanbul are the stuff of romance.

ras el hanout

Mostly identified with Moroccan cooking, but found in other parts of North Africa, ras el hanout means 'top of the shop'. It is a mixture that varies from shop to shop and cook to cook – a pinch of this and a pinch of that. The mixture below is a popular one, but you can vary it according to the flavours you like best – try turmeric, nigella, saffron, pepper, cardamom, coriander, cloves, lavender and, if you can get them, ash berries, grains of paradise or monk's pepper.

1 teaspoon cardamom seeds (not pods)

1 blade of mace or ½ teaspoon ground mace (optional)

1 teaspoon cubeb (optional) or peppercorns

3 allspice berries

½ cinnamon stick

a large pinch of saffron threads

1 teaspoon freshly grated nutmeg

1 teaspoon ground ginger

2–3 unsprayed dried rosebuds, torn into small pieces

Toast the whole spices in a dry frying pan over low heat until aromatic, then stir in the nutmeg, ginger and rose petals. Store in an airtight container. Just before using, grind to a powder with a mortar and pestle.

zahtar

A simple blend used to flavour breads and vegetables throughout the Middle East, but particularly in the Gulf, the Levant, Turkey and North Africa.

1 tablespoon crushed dried thyme

1 tablespoon sumac

2 tablespoons lightly toasted sesame seeds

Mix all the ingredients together. Store in an airtight container.

baharat

Also known as *bezar*, this is the major spice blend of the Gulf States. The spices vary slightly and the mix carries local names. As in other spice blends of the Middle East and parts of Africa, the Indian influence is strong.

1 small piece of cinnamon or cassia bark

½ teaspoon cardamom seeds (not pods)

1 teaspoon whole cloves (about 20)

½ teaspoon black peppercorns

1 teaspoon coriander seeds

½ teaspoon ground turmeric

about ¼ teaspoon freshly grated nutmeg

1½ teaspoons sweet smoked paprika

¼ teaspoon chilli powder

Grind the spices to a fine powder: if you like, you can toast them in a dry frying pan first. Store in an airtight container.

harissa

This very hot Tunisian spice paste can be bought in tubes and jars – or by the ladle in North African delicatessens. It has a smoky, fiery flavour and can be added to stews, grills, chickpeas or other foods. It is also served as a condiment with couscous.

½ teaspoon caraway seeds

1½ teaspoons coriander seeds

¾ teaspoon cumin seeds

4–5 hot dried red chillies, deseeded and soaked in warm water

1 garlic clove, crushed

3 tablespoons extra virgin olive oil

a pinch of sea salt

Toast the whole seeds in a dry frying pan over low heat for a few minutes until aromatic. Grind coarsely, then transfer to a food processor or blender and add the chillies, garlic, oil and salt. Blend to a thick paste and store in the refrigerator.

ethiopian berbere

This mixture is from the Horn of Africa. It requires fenugreek, chillies and coriander, but, similarly to South Indian masalas, the other spices may vary slightly from home to home. Berbere is used in wats (traditional Ethiopian stews).

1 teaspoon fenugreek seeds

10 medium-to-large dried red chillies

1 teaspoon coriander seeds

1 teaspoon cardamom seeds (not pods)

5 black peppercorns

5 whole cloves

2 small pieces of cinnamon or cassia

2 teaspoons ground ginger

Roast the whole spices in a dry frying pan over low heat for a few minutes, until aromatic. Grind to a fine powder, then add the ginger and blend well. Store in an airtight container.

egyptian dukka

A strongly flavoured nut and spice mix used around the Eastern Mediterranean. It is eaten with bread as a starter or dry dip and is also good sprinkled into yoghurt or over salads. This recipe contains a dash of sugar to soften the flavour, but you could leave it out for authenticity. For a more fiery dukka, add some chilli flakes.

75 g shelled hazelnuts, chopped

25 g sesame seeds

25 g cumin seeds

½ teaspoon dried marjoram

¼ teaspoon dried thyme

½ teaspoon freshly grated lemon zest

a pinch of light brown sugar (optional)

sea salt and freshly ground black pepper

Put the nuts and seeds into a dry frying pan and toast until aromatic, then add the remaining ingredients. Store in an airtight container.

south asian spice mixes

The people of the Indian subcontinent could not survive without their multifarious spice mixtures. Each region has its own blends, as does each community. There are different blends for different kinds of foods, and blends that are unique to each family, handed down from mother to daughter. A typical mortar is often round or rectangular, and the pestle is like a short, thick, stone rolling pin. It is well worth making your own spice mixes, as commercial spice mixes are often disappointing.

tarka spice-fry

The tarka is the backbone of Indian spicing and is a method of releasing the flavour of the spices by frying them in hot fat. Heat a small amount of oil or ghee, add the spices and fry briefly. Tarkas can be mixed through raita (yoghurt dip) or dhaal (lentil sauce), or used at the beginning of a dish, before other ingredients are added and cooked. Here are a few of the most widely used tarkas.

- Simple tarka: ground turmeric, chilli powder and cumin seeds.
- Pulow tarka: cinnamon stick, cloves, cardamom pods, peppercorns, bay leaves and, for a yellow pulow, turmeric.
- North Indian/Pakistani tarkas: black cardamom pods, cinnamon stick and black cumin seeds or cloves; or green cardamom pods, cumin seeds and cloves.
- Punjabi tarka: nigella seeds, turmeric, fenugreek seeds and chilli powder.
- South Indian/Sri Lankan tarkas: curry leaves, mustard seeds, asafoetida, ground turmeric and chilli powder or chillies, with channa (yellow) or urid (white) lentils; or cumin and mustard seeds, turmeric and green chillies; or red chillies, fenugreek and mustard seeds.

punjabi garam masala

Garam means 'hot' and *masala* means 'spice' and there are numerous variations on this spice blend originally from northern India, of which there are many regional variations. Most do not require the spices to be dry-roasted first, although some cooks do prefer to dry-roast.

2 tablespoons cumin seeds
2 teaspoons black cumin seeds
seeds from 2 green cardamom pods
2 black cardamom pods
5-cm piece of cinnamon stick
5 whole cloves
2 bay leaves

Using a mortar and pestle, mini-blender or spice grinder, grind all the spices to a fine powder. Store in an airtight container.

Variations To make Pakistani garam masala, add fennel and coriander seeds to the above mixture. Kashmiri garam masala is similar to Pakistani, but without the green cardamom and with mace, and sometimes saffron, added.

baath masala

A highly fragrant mixture for South Indian spiced rice with vegetables or herbs. When buying the lentils, make sure you ask for channa and urid split lentils, not whole lentils.

50 g channa dhaal (yellow lentils)
75 g urid dhaal (white lentils)
7 medium dried red chillies (not Thai bird's eye)
9 whole cloves
1 cardamom pod
2 cinnamon sticks, broken into small pieces
4 tablespoons unsweetened desiccated coconut
4 tablespoons coriander seeds

Put the channa dhaal into a frying pan and dry-roast over medium heat for about 30 seconds, stirring all the time. Add the urid dhaal, dried red chillies, cloves, cardamom pod, broken cinnamon sticks, desiccated coconut and coriander seeds. Dry-roast, stirring constantly, until you can smell a toasted aroma and steam begins rising from the pan. The lentils in particular should be roasted nicely.

Transfer the mixture to a mortar and pestle, mini-blender or spice grinder. Grind coarsely and set aside until ready for use.

ginger, garlic and chilli paste

This wet paste is used in many dishes. Sometimes onions are blended with the other ingredients, or they may be added in chopped form, or sometimes not at all. Often, ginger and chillies are pounded together on their own; especially by communities that eschew garlic.

3 cm fresh ginger, peeled and chopped

2 green chillies, chopped

2 garlic cloves, chopped

Using a mortar and pestle or a small blender, grind the ingredients together, adding a dash of water or oil if necessary. (Don't add too much water – the paste should be thick.) Use fresh, or make it a day in advance and refrigerate.

sarina (rasam pudi)

Pudi means 'powder', and this spice mix is used to make the dhaal, tomato and tamarind soup known as *saru* or the thin, dhaal-less version to drink, called *rasam*. *Rasa* means 'liquid or essence' and this is very much the essence of South India.

3 teaspoons sunflower oil

½ teaspoon asafoetida

1 tablespoon black peppercorns

1 tablespoon cumin seeds

1 tablespoon black mustard seeds

1 tablespoon fenugreek seeds (methi)

50 g coriander seeds

5 fresh curry leaves

¼ teaspoon ground turmeric

25 g large dried red chillies

Heat 1 teaspoon of the oil in a frying pan, add the asafoetida and black pepper, and toast, stirring, then set aside. Next, toast the cumin, then the mustard seeds, then the fenugreek, setting them aside as you go. Heat another teaspoon of oil and fry the coriander seeds and curry leaves. Transfer to a plate and add the turmeric.

Heat the remaining oil and fry the chillies. Grind all the ingredients to a fine powder. Store in an airtight container.

chai masala

Chai means 'tea' and it is taken on its own, with snacks – constantly! Always served with milk and sugar, it is a much-loved elixir. Chai masala is tea infused with spices. If you want to be truly Indian in your endeavours, froth the chai as the chaiwallahs do, pouring the hot liquid from a great height from one steel *lota* (tumbler) to another.

1 cinnamon stick, halved

4 whole cloves

6 cardamom pods

2 blades of mace

2 cassia buds, black peppercorns

a pinch of freshly grated nutmeg

a pinch of ground ginger

4–5 teaspoons Assam or Nilgiri tea leaves

250 ml milk

sugar or honey, to taste

Put the spices and 1 litre water in a saucepan and bring to the boil. Reduce the heat, cover and simmer gently for 5 minutes. Add the tea leaves and brew for 1 minute, then add the milk. Stir and continue to brew to required strength (4 more minutes is perfect). Strain and serve with sugar or honey to taste, or froth from pan to pan or, if you have the knack, from tumbler to tumbler!

east asian spice mixes

Though not as numerous as the blends of South and South-east Asia, those of East Asia are subtle and exotic. Spice mixes, such as Chinese five-spice powder and Japanese shichimi togarashi, regularly appear in the domestic kitchens. Many East Asian spice mixes include ginger and black and white sesame seeds as well as other flavourings, such as dried tangerine peel, liquorice root and dried seaweed. Chinese spices are also linked to medicinal use.

shichimi togarashi

A ubiquitous Japanese spice mix, widely available in supermarkets. This blend of seven spices includes the unusual flavours of sansho, yuzo (dried citrus peel) and nori (dried seaweed). It is often sprinkled over soups. Sometimes other seeds like hemp or rape are used, as well as shisho herb.

½ teaspoon white or black poppy seeds

½ teaspoon black sesame seeds

1 teaspoon white sesame seeds

1 teaspoon chilli powder

1½–2 teaspoons ground sansho

1½ teaspoons dried yuzo flakes

few pieces of nori or mixed dried sea vegetables, such as dulse and sea lettuce, crushed

Put all the ingredients into an airtight container, stir well, then store in a cool, dark place.

szechuan seasoning

Very easy to make, this spiced and toasted Chinese salt seasoning is used to sprinkle over foods. It is also excellent as a dip for dim sum snack foods and other party foods.

1 teaspoon coarse salt

½ tablespoon Szechuan peppercorns

1 teaspoon Chinese five-spice powder

Put the salt and Szechuan peppercorns into a dry frying pan and toast gently until both begin to brown (take care because they burn easily). Remove from the heat, let cool, grind to a powder and mix in the five-spice powder.

chinese five-spice powder

This essential Chinese blend is made with a minimum of five spices – the first five are listed below – but some blends may also contain extras spices, such as ground ginger or coriander. It should be very fragrant, with star anise dominating.

1 teaspoon Szechuan peppercorns, black seeds discarded

1 whole star anise

¾ teaspoon fennel seeds

½ teaspoon whole cloves (about 10)

2 pieces cinnamon stick or cassia bark, about 5 cm long

¼ teaspoon ground ginger

Put the Szechuan peppercorns in a dry frying pan and toast briefly. Using a spice grinder or a mortar and pestle, grind the peppercorns, star anise, fennel seeds, cloves and cinnamon, then stir in the ground ginger. Store in an airtight container.

south-east asian spice mixes

South-east Asian spice mixes are a subtle blend of salt and sweet, sour and spicy. The Asian penchant for fire began with ginger, galangal and pepper, but when the chilli arrived, everything changed. Now the variety and sheer heat of Asian chillies is staggering. Because spices in this region are usually fresh, the mixtures are often in paste or liquid form.

thai green curry paste

This mild green curry paste is made from spices and herbs; if you wish to be true to its roots, feel free to use many more chillies.

1 tablespoon grated kaffir lime zest
or regular lime zest

4–5 green bird's eye chillies,
deseeded and chopped

several lemon balm leaves (optional), chopped

1 stalk of lemongrass, outer leaves discarded,
the remainder very finely chopped

¾ teaspoon coriander seeds, toasted
in a dry frying pan

25 g coriander leaves, chopped

50 g coriander stems and roots, chopped

2–3 garlic cloves, chopped

2 spring onions, chopped

3 cm fresh galangal or ginger,
peeled and chopped

3 tablespoons Thai fish sauce

Using a food processor or mortar and pestle, grind all the ingredients to a thick, chunky paste. If using a food processor, add a little water to keep the blades turning if necessary.

thai red curry paste

This paste is fierce in colour and heat, although you can decrease or increase the chillies according to taste.

8–10 red bird's eye chillies,
deseeded and chopped

a small piece of toasted shrimp paste
(see note, page 24) or 1 teaspoon anchovy
paste plus a dash of Thai fish sauce

1 tablespoon grated kaffir lime or regular
lime zest

1 stalk of lemongrass, outer leaves discarded,
remainder very finely chopped

1 teaspoon cumin seeds, toasted
in a dry frying pan

1 teaspoon white or black peppercorns

1 tablespoon coriander seeds,
toasted in a dry frying pan

2–3 garlic cloves, chopped

3 cm fresh galangal or ginger,
peeled and chopped

3 tablespoons chopped shallots or onions

1–2 tablespoons finely chopped coriander root

Using a food processor or mortar and pestle, grind all the ingredients to a thick, chunky paste. If using a food processor, add a little water to keep the blades turning if necessary.

vietnamese tamarind dip

This South-east Asian dip has that wonderful sour flavour unique to tamarind. You can also use this as a dressing.

75 g lump tamarind or 1 teaspoon
tamarind paste

2 teaspoons groundnut oil

1–2 teaspoons Vietnamese or Thai fish sauce

1 large garlic clove, crushed

1 teaspoon jaggery (unrefined palm sugar)
or brown sugar

a dash of freshly squeezed lime juice (optional)

To prepare the lump tamarind, put it in a small bowl with 200 ml hot water. Let soak for 15 minutes. Squeeze the tamarind through your fingers in the water and continue until all of it has been squeezed into a pulp, then press through a sieve.

Put 3 tablespoons of the prepared tamarind, or 1 teaspoon of paste, into a small bowl, then whisk in the groundnut oil and fish sauce, add the garlic and jaggery and stir until dissolved. Add a dash of lime juice, if using, then serve.

(Any remaining tamarind paste can be boiled in a saucepan, left to cool and refrigerated for later use.)

herb & spice directory

Ajowan *(Carum ajowan* or *Trachyspermum ammi)*
Native to Asia and Africa; also known as ajwain. Tiny seeds with a slightly bitter, thyme-like flavour, used whole or ground, valued as a digestive and often partnered with gram (chickpea) flour in snacks like pakora. Available from Indian, Pakistani and Bangladeshi shops, but if you can't find it you could substitute a little crushed dried thyme.

Allspice *(Pimenta dioica)*
Native to the Caribbean and Central America. Its name reflects its fruity, peppery mixture of clove, nutmeg and cinnamon flavours; also known as Jamaica pepper. Allspice is a brown-red berry used in pickles, marinades, soups and stews. Ground, it is used to season meats and is a component of European mixed spice, which is used in cakes, biscuits and puddings.

Amchoor *(Mangifera indica)*
The mango is native to India; amchoor is ground from dried unripe mangoes. It gives an excellent sour flavour; often part of chaat masala mixes used for snacks and salads. For sourness, you could also use *anardana* (below) or, in a pinch, lemon juice. Tamarind would be a better substitute. Available from Indian, Pakistani and Bangladeshi shops.

Anardana *(Punica granatum)*
The pomegranate is valued as a fruit and for its syrup in the Middle East and Asia. Dried ground pomegranate seeds, called *anardana* in India, are used for their sour flavour. You could substitute amchoor or tamarind. Available from Indian, Pakistani and Bangladeshi shops.

Annatto (Achiote/Achuete) *(Bixa orellana)*
Native to South America. Bright red seeds mainly used as a colouring agent – for example for cheese – but also ground and used as a spice in Mexico and parts of South America. The taste is nutty and slightly tart. Available from Mexican and Filipino shops.

Anise/Aniseed *(Pimpinella anisum)*
Native to the Mediterranean region. The pale brown, ridged seeds have a liquorice flavour and are used whole or ground. Since anise has such a distinctive flavour, a number of other spices are described as having an 'anise' note. In Europe they flavour pastis, ouzo and other anise-based drinks. Anise seeds are used in baked goods and confectionery.

Asafoetida *(Ferula asafoetida)*
Native to Persia and Afghanistan. Prized in Roman cooking, but now used only in western and southern India. A resin, mostly sold ground and sometimes in lumps, it is unpleasantly pungent in scent, but fabulous when cooked with other spices to flavour regional Indian dishes. It is often used by onion and garlic-eschewing Brahmins for its strong flavour. Available in Indian, Pakistani and Bangladeshi shops and some supermarkets. Should be used in small doses.

Assam gelugor *(Garcinia atroviridis)*
Very sour flavouring, used dried and sliced in South-east Asian cooking, especially in seafood dishes. Thai *madan (G. schomburgkiana)* has a similar sour taste and is used fresh or dried in Thailand. Difficult to find outside Asia.

Basil *(Ocimum basilicum)*
Native to India, where it is sacred (see below). Basil was first brought to Egypt around 3000 years ago, then on to Rome and so to all parts of southern Europe. It takes its name from the Greek *basileus*, meaning 'king'. These days it grows wherever the climate suits. The common basil we know as sweet or Italian basil is not shy about throwing its peppery, minty clove-like scent around when warmed by the sun, but when cold in the confines of the larder it can smell of cats. Many cooks have a rule that basil must only be torn, not cut. Metal reacts with the plant juices, turning the cut edges black and bitter. If the leaf is torn, the tear takes the natural line of the cell structure. There are two types of Thai sweet basil available from Thai and other Asian markets. One has a smooth pale purple stalk with deep green, very sprightly, shiny leaves, squat purple flowers and a strong anise and liquorice aroma and flavour. The other has a brighter green leaf with a tangy, slightly lemony flavour and usually white or pale pink flowers. The latter is often used with fish. The edges of the leaves are smooth on both sweet basils.

Greek or bush basil *(O. b.* var. *minimum)* is very bushy with tiny pointed leaves and white flowers. It is grown throughout Greece in gardens or pots near doorways as a sign of welcome and in churches it can be found just below the altar in its spiritual role as holy basil.

Lettuce basil *(O. b.* var. *crispum)* is a large-leaved variety. Use whole leaves in wrappings or as stuffings, or tear them into salads.

Purple basil *(O. b.* var. *purpurascens)*, also known as opal basil, has pinkish-purple, and in some cases almost black, leaves. If it flops, plunge into hand-hot water for 15 minutes – not only does this bring it back to life, it intensifies its colour quite dramatically.

Holy basil *(O. sanctum)*, also known as Tulsi, is the sacred herb of Hindu India and believed to be Krishna's favourite plant above any garden flower. It is used as a religious offering rather than in cooking, although it is used to make a delicious tisane. There are two types of Thai holy basil available from Thai and Asian stores. The most common is the one with pale green, slightly floppy leaves, best wilted into dishes at the last moment when its subtler flavour can come to the fore. When the leaves are squeezed the aroma is very similar to that of engine oil. The other holy basil has darker leaves, pinky-purple on the top of the leaf, with deep-pink flowers. The flavour is minty and camphoric and deliciously fragrant when heated. Both these holy basils have a slightly serrated leaf.

Bay leaves *(Laurus nobilis)*
Native to the Mediterranean, where it still thrives pungently and powerfully. Greek and Roman heroes were crowned with wreaths of bay leaves as a symbol of excellence. When you crush the leaves, the aromas range from grassy and floral to bitter – as a flavouring herb, they stand up to long cooking, which brings out their sweet mellowness. Infuse a leaf or two in milk and cream for savoury or sweet dishes or use a sprig in a bowl of red wine marinade with garlic and onions. When cooking cabbage, cauliflower or other strong-smelling vegetables, add a bay leaf to diminish the odour.

Black cumin *(Cuminum nigrum)*
Native to North India, Kashmir, Pakistan, Iran and Afghanistan. Known as *kala jeera*; thin blackish seeds which are less bitter than regular cumin. Much valued in the above regions as a whole spice or as part of spice mixtures, such as Punjabi Garam Masala (page 176). Sold in Indian, Pakistani and Bangladeshi shops.

Borage *(Borago officinalis)*
Borage was taken all over Europe by the Roman legions. The soldiers believed it gave them great courage – something obviously worked, as they rampaged their way across the known world for over 500 years. Young, fresh borage has strong cucumber-flavoured leaves, which are delicious dipped in light batter and deep-fried. Float the star-like purple flowers in drinks or freeze them in ice cubes to chill summer drinks – a classic when served with that English favourite, Pimm's.

Brown cardamom *(Amomum subulatum)*
Native to India. Not a true cardamom, but a slightly larger brown pod with coarser flavour. Also known as black cardamom. Used in Kashmir, North India and Pakistan as a whole spice and ground in some masalas. Sold in Indian, Pakistani and Bangladeshi shops.

Burnet *(Poterium sanguisorba)*
Native to Europe. Also known as salad burnet, this pretty herb has fine-toothed green leaves. It is best used when young, as the leaves from older plants can be tough. It was a common ingredient in Elizabethan times and is still used in France and Italy in butters and sauces, such as Chivry (page 169).

Caraway *(Carum carvi)*
Native to Asia and northern and central Europe. Caraway is often confused with cumin but has a stronger anise note, especially when cooked. In Europe the small, thin brown seeds are used to flavour pickles, sauerkraut, cabbage dishes, bread and cheese. It is also great with sour cream. It is popular in Turkey and used in harissa in Tunisia.

Cardamom *(Elettaria cardamomum)*
Native to southern India and Sri Lanka. A 'luxury' spice with a unique, exotic scent. Pale green oval pods (white cardamoms are bleached green ones) with tiny black seeds. Brown cardamom is a different species (see above). Whole pods may be used, bruised to release the scent, or just the seeds – whole or ground to a powder. (Whole pods are also crushed to a powder, but that of the seeds alone is 'sweeter'.) Cardamom is used extensively in South Asia in both sweet and savoury dishes, alone or in spice mixtures. It is also used as coffee flavouring in the Middle East, and in Finnish baking.

Cassia *(Cinnamomum cassia)*
Native to China. The Latin name reflects its similarity to true cinnamon, although cassia is not as delicate or sweetly scented. Often sold as broken pieces of bark, or ground to a powder, it is widely used in China, South-east Asia and the United States. Cassia buds are the small, brown, dried unripe fruits of the cassia tree with their stalks. They are used whole in China for pickles and to flavour other dishes, and are used ground in some South Asian spice mixes.
They are difficult to find, but are sometimes available from South Asian shops and specialist spice outlets.

Cayenne pepper (*see* **Chilli**)

Celery *(Apium graveolens)*
Native to Europe. Celery was developed from smallage, or wild celery, during the 17th century. There are many varieties of celery, including some grown for the root, known as celeriac. Celery leaf is available in pots from garden centres and is used to flavour soups and salads. The tiny brown seeds have a strong and slightly bitter celery flavour. They are most commonly used ground in celery salt and in some American spice blends.

Chervil *(Anthriscus cerefolium)*
was introduced as a flavouring herb to Western Europe by the invading Roman legions. They carried it from the Caucasus and the Middle East to western Europe where it settled into common use, especially in France and Belgium. It is part of the herb quartet that flavours the classic French dish *omelette au fines herbes*, to which its contribution is important, because a little chervil accentuates the flavour of the other three herbs. It makes a delicate soup and when added to young carrots, it reaches dizzy heights. Always add chervil to a hot dish at the very last moment because its flavour is destroyed by prolonged cooking. Use the tangles of lacy leaves in salads to maximize invaluable nutritional benefits. Chervil has a sweet, mildly anise flavour with a twang of fruity wine. Though it looks delicate, it's a brave little herb and when grown in the garden is a good deal hardier than any commercially grown specimen. It was available from supermarkets for a while, but the poor little thing wasn't quite strong enough for the tough packaged life. You can find it in good greengrocers who know how to deal with its delicate demeanour.

Chilli, Paprika *(Capsicum annuum, C. chinense, C. frutescens)*
Native to Central and South America and the Caribbean; most of the world's chilli cultivars descend from the above species. Pods vary in colour, shape and size: red, orange or green; long and thin or bonnet-shaped; 2–20 cm long; strength ranges from mild to fierce. Seeds can be removed to reduce ferocity. Dried chillies may be sold whole, crushed or ground to a powder; cayenne pepper is a fiery variety, paprika is milder. Hungarian paprika and the smoked Spanish version (pimentón) are superior to most commercial paprika. There are two kinds of pimentón; hot and sweet. They are both oak-smoked, the best supposedly being produced in Extremadura in south-west Spain. Sold in small square cans with resealable lids to seal in flavour and scent.

Chinese keys *(Boesenbergia pandurata)*; **Kencur** *(Kaempferia galanga);* **Zedoary** *(Curcuma zedoaria)*
Native to South-east Asia. These are all rhizomes from the ginger family with similar ginger/galangal-like flavours. Some are spicy, some fragrant, some bitter. Chinese keys (krachai) is the most individual in shape and its lemon/ginger flavour is used in Thai cooking. They can be difficult to find outside Asia, except in some Chinese and South-east Asian shops.

Chives *(Allium schoenoprasum)*
Brought back to Europe from the East by Marco Polo in the 13th century, chives have become indispensable in the kitchen, in the same way as garlic and onions. They are a perfect flavouring for soufflés and savoury tarts with fillings based on eggs, cream or cheese and are delicious with baked or new potatoes. If you're a gardener, there are many varieties available, some with white flowers, but the common chive with its lilac-pink pompom flower heads is hard to beat. The flowers can be scattered over salads and grilled dishes or any dish where a hint of onion flavour works. After cutting the leaves from the plant, wrap them in damp kitchen paper, then put them in a plastic bag and store in the salad drawer of the refrigerator.

Chinese chives *(A. tuberosum)*, or garlic chives, have been cultivated for centuries in China, Japan and Vietnam. One variety has flat leaves and is sold either with just leaves, or with the large buds or flowers. Chinese chives give a mild garlic flavour and can be used like common chives or in stir-fries and rice dishes. These can be bought from Asian stores bound in long bundles. In some Chinese markets, you will find a variety that is blanched under cloches to whiten them, and these are considered a delicacy. Flowering chives (kuchai) are grown specifically for their flowering stems, both in bud and flower form. The stems and flowers are chopped into stir-fry dishes. These have an ultra-powerful, pungently garlic smell, which resembles wild garlic, but cooking tempers the smell and flavour.

Cinnamon *(Cinnamomum verum* or *C. zeylanicum)*
Native to Sri Lanka (formerly Ceylon). The brown 'quills' are the rolled-up inner bark of an

evergreen tree and are used whole or ground. Prized around the world for its sweet woody fragrance and taste. Cinnamon graces sweet foods in the West; elsewhere it enriches savoury foods, from tagines to biryanis.

Cloves ***(Eugenia caryophyllata*** **or** ***Syzygium aromaticum)***
Native to the Maluku Islands (formerly Moluccas), Indonesia. Cloves are the unopened flower buds of an evergreen tree, dried and used whole or ground, as well as in spice mixtures. They are dark reddish-brown with a sultry scent and slightly bitter flavour – numbing when tasted alone. Cloves are used in baking and in savoury foods, such as in pulows, or pressed into onions to flavour stocks or stews, or into hams before they are baked.

Coriander ***(Coriandrum sativum)***
Native to the Mediterranean and West Asia. Coriander is mentioned in the Bible and in Sanskrit texts and was found in Egyptian tombs in seed form. It was brought to Europe by late bronze-age nomads to flavour their barley gruel, while the Spaniards carried it to Mexico and Peru, where it became an indispensable partner to their much loved chilli. In Britain, it was commercially grown in the 19th century for the seed, which was used as a supporting flavour for gin. Although fresh coriander must not be cooked to death, it really needs that brief assignation with the warmth of the food to bring out its fullness. On the other hand, its idiosyncratic flavour in fresh salsa is not to be missed. Ground coriander has a nutty taste with a surprising scent of orange and it comes into its own when toasted. It is commonly paired with cumin in ground blends and pastes in South and South-east Asia and is also used whole as a pickling spice.

Cubeb ***(Piper cubeba)***
Cubeb belongs to the same family as black pepper. The dark brown berries are like black peppercorns with a stalk or 'tail'. The flavour falls between allspice and black pepper, either of which could be substituted. Available from specialist shops and some mail order sources.

Cumin ***(Cuminum cyminum)***
Native to the eastern Mediterranean but widespread since antiquity. Pungent, nutty and warm with a hint of bitterness. The seeds resemble caraway and the best flavour emerges from them when toasted. It is widely used in North Africa, the Middle East, South Asia and Mexico. The seeds flavour oil in India and ground cumin is added to meat, vegetable and bean dishes. Cumin is an important element of spice mixtures in many countries.

Curry leaf ***(Murraya koenigii)***
A musky, spicy, aromatic leaf and not, as its name implies, anything like curry powder, although it is used as a component of Sri Lankan curry powder. These leaves are from a deciduous tree that grows wild in parts of India, Thailand and Sri Lanka. It's cultivated in southern India where it's popular in many dishes. Here, it is often known as *kari patta* and used as part of a *tarka*, which is a fried mixture that also includes cumin seed, dried chillies and the spice, asafoetida, added to a dish at the end of cooking. Curry leaves are most often used to flavour dishes rather than being eaten. Available from Indian and Asian stores in sealed packs. The thin stalks have about 14 small bright, shiny, green leaves that will keep in the refrigerator quite well for weeks. They freeze well, too.

Dill ***(Anethum graveolens)***
Dill was grown in the Middle East in biblical times and later migrated with travellers into Europe, North and South America, further east into Asia as well as north to Scandinavia. Its name comes appropriately from the old Norse word *dylla* meaning 'to lull'. The leaves have a sweet, almost alcoholic flavour, with vague hints of anise that aren't as strong as fennel, but similar to caraway in taste. Dill is used in Scandinavia with salmon, carrots and beetroot or tossed into new potatoes with butter. Polish cooks use it with sour cream, hard-boiled eggs and gherkins. The Greeks like to partner it with broad beans and in Iran it's eaten raw, along with other herbs on the table throughout the meal. Dill is used as a vegetable in South-east Asia, where it's always cooked and goes by the name *paksi* or *pak chi lao*. Dill seeds are small, flattish and beige with a lightly pungent flavour. They are used as a pickling spice, especially in Scandinavia and Russia, and to flavour bread, potatoes and sometimes pastries. They are also used in breads in South Asia.

Epazote ***(Chenopodium ambrosiodes)***
Native to the Americas, where it grows so enthusiastically it is viewed almost as a weed. It has a pungent flavour and is often used with beans, due to its reputation as a carminative – the ability to reduce the flatulent effect of beans. Its other name, wormseed, explains its other medicinal use. Epazote is the important flavour in *papadzutes*, fresh corn tortillas rolled with a filling of hard-boiled eggs and swathed in a pumpkin seed sauce called *mole verde*. The leaves give off an odorous and pungent hemp-like smell when squeezed. It works well in stews and with pulses, and can also be used raw in salsas. It is available as a seed so you can grow it yourself.

Fennel ***(Foeniculum vulgare)***
Native to southern Europe. Fennel has a feathery foliage under an umbrella of yellow flowers. It was used by in ancient Greece to suppress the appetite. Fennel has an aniseed-like scent and flavour and is the perfect herb stuffed inside or sprinkled on top of oily fish. The clean, fresh flavour is delicious tossed through char-grilled vegetables. It will keep in a plastic bag in the salad drawer of the refrigerator for four days providing it's not wet, when it becomes slimy very quickly. Fennel seeds are flat, oval-shaped and a yellowy green and go well with pork.

Fenugreek ***(Trigonella foenum-graecum)***
Native to the eastern Mediterranean region. The yellowish seeds have a strong aroma, often encountered when opening ready-made curry powders. Hence people think of fenugreek as smelling of curry powder, but it is the other way around! It should be used in small quantities, especially if ground. It is popular in Ethiopia, Yemen and Afghanistan, as well as in South Asia. The bushy, silvery, olive-green leaves, known as methi, have a nutty, pungent, sweet curry aroma and tightly budded pale ivory flowers. It grows a little like its relative, clover. In Iran where it's a popular ingredient, it is called *shambaleeleh* or *shambalides* meaning 'clover-like vegetable'. In the Lebanon it is known as *halbeh*. In Yemen and Ethiopia it is a staple vegetable. Fresh bunches of fenugreek will keep in a plastic bag in the salad drawer of the refrigerator for up to five days. Available from South Asian, Ethiopian and Middle Eastern shops.

Galangal ***(Alpinia galanga)***
Native to South-east Asia. A rhizome of the ginger family, generally known as 'greater galangal', it has a ginger-like flavour and aroma, but tangier, with hints of lemongrass. Used fresh throughout South-east Asia to flavour curries and soups. Available from South-east Asian shops – as dried pieces, as a powder and, if you're lucky, fresh.

Lesser galangal *(A. officinarum)* is native to China and widely used in South-east Asia. Its flavour resembles ginger and black pepper.

Garlic *(Allium sativum)*
Garlic was cultivated in the Mediterranean by the Ancient Egyptians. It is the ultimate herb, grown for flavouring and as a vegetable in its own right and used in many parts of the world, including Europe, Asia, the Middle East, Africa and Latin America. The active substance in garlic is ailicun, which comes to the fore when the cloves are chopped or crushed, this is the medicinally active part and creates the garlic odour. Garlic is at its most beneficial to health when eaten raw, but still retains many benefits when cooked. Russians eat it to keep old age at bay. If you grow your own, divide the cloves from the bulb and plant them in autumn for the next year. They produce a delicious crop, and also keep insects away from other plants. Young green garlic is useful in many dishes for its mild flavour and also makes a delicious soup. Extreme temperature change can cause garlic to take on a hotter taste. The variety grown in Thailand has a less pungent flavour than its Western relative. Leave some plants to flower – they are beautiful with large pompoms, like big chive flowers.

Wild garlic *(A. ursinum)*, or ramsons, has spear-like leaves and is found growing wild in muddy, shady places. Take care when gathering it, and wash thoroughly before use. It is also cultivated and, in season, is sometimes sold in gourmet stores. Both flowers and leaves are edible, but the leaves are best eaten before the plant flowers. The leaves are lovely as a wrapping for steamed fish. The stunning starry flowers have a pungent flavour and are good used in a salad of bitter leaves tossed with goats' cheese and nuts. Chop and wilt the leaves with baby spinach to fold through stuffed pasta just before serving.

Geranium *(Pelargonium)*
Native to southern Africa. Geranium leaves have an intense scent associated with the individual varieties. Edible varieties include rose *(P. 'Graveolens')*, lemon *(P. crispum)*, apple *(P. odoratissimum)*, peppermint *(P. tomentosum)* and nutmeg *(P. 'Fragrans')*. The flowers, unlike other herbs, have no scent at all but are edible and can be used to decorate puddings or salads. Use the fresh leaves to scent sugar stored in a jar – the results can be used for custards, syrups, meringues, ice creams and jellies. The leaves are pretty pressed into the top of a cake and covered with a dusting of caster sugar before baking.

Ginger *(Zingiber officinale)*
Native to South-east Asia, ginger is now widely grown, from Jamaica to Japan. A rhizome with many 'fingers', ginger has a refreshing flavour with a hot kick. It can be used fresh, dried or ground, in sweet and savoury dishes. Fresh ginger is most esteemed for stir-fries, spice pastes and as tea, while ground ginger is popular in baking. 'Stem ginger', preserved in syrup, is used for puddings.

Grains of paradise/Melegueta pepper/Guinea pepper *(Amomum* or *Afromomum melegueta)*
Native to West Africa. These peppery brown seeds are from a plant related to cardamom. This spice was important in medieval Europe, but is now confined to West and North African cooking. Sometimes available through specialist spice shops and mail order sources.

Hyssop *(Hyssopus officinalis)*
A common Mediterranean shrub, hyssop was a sacred herb in ancient Greece. It is a good foil for rich pork dishes and oily fish because it aids digestion. The leaves have a minty, anise-like flavour with a little sage note, while the white, pink or purple flowers have a minty taste. The leaves are still quite potent in winter and add a warm spiciness to poached fruits. When chopped and used as a rub, its strength is the perfect partner for game dishes. But take care – like all the woody herbs, its strength varies depending on the season, and a heavy hand can ruin a dish.

Japanese shiso/perilla *(Perilla frutescens)*
Related to the basil and mint family, shiso is as common in Japan as mint is in the West. There are many varieties – some nettle-like and some quite frilly. It has a mild, sweet, cumin-like aroma and the first taste you get is similar. The afterburn is a minty spicy flavour. Its main use in Japan is in sashimi, where it is said to protect against any parasites that may be in the raw fish. Green shiso is also used to make sushi maki. The cultivated red shiso is used to colour the umeboshi sour plums and is used to garnish beefsteaks, this is perhaps why it is often called the beefsteak plant, although this may also be due to its deep red colour. The seeds are also sprouted in pots, creating red and green cress-like sprouts, which are great for salads. The leaves and flowering tips make wonderful herb tempura and are also delicious sliced into rice and salads. Shiso is also used in Korean and Vietnamese cuisines.

Juniper berries *(Juniperus communis)*
Native to Europe and North America. Purple-black berries with a strong, aromatic, bitter-sweet flavour. Excellent with game, pork and other meats, they appear in sausages, pâtés, terrines, marinades, sauces and sauerkraut. Both gin's name and flavour derive from juniper.

Kaffir lime leaves *(Citrus hystrix)*
Native to South-east Asia. These are the beautiful dark, glossy green leaves found in Thai curry spice packs and sold in bags in Asian markets. You can freeze what you don't use immediately and use straight from frozen. The leaves grow in pairs – bruise and use whole, removing before serving, or slice very finely and grind with a mortar and pestle. The word kaffir is old Hindi meaning 'foreign'. They are also known as makrut.

Kokum *(Garcinia indica)*
A sticky black flavouring, derived from a tropical Asian fruit, with a tamarind-like sour taste. Used only in Western Indian cooking, especially in fish dishes; sometimes called fish tamarind. Some Indian shops stock it, and sometimes available by mail order.

Laksa leaf (*see* Vietnamese coriander)

Lavender *(Lavendula angustifolia)*
Native to the Mediterranean. Highly prized by the Greeks and Romans, who liked the scent and healing qualities in their bath water, its name is derived from the Latin *lavare* meaning 'to wash'. The culinary talents of lavender have been known for centuries and it's becoming a top herb again. Use the flowers to flavour sugar and to make biscuits, syrups, ice creams and in a more savoury context for stuffings and sauces. Use the leaves to flavour game and roast with a leg of lamb as you would rosemary. It's very potent, so use it sparingly. The fresh blossoms can be scattered over summer strawberries along with a dusting of scented sugar (the berries can take the overkill) and a dollop of whipped cream.

Lemon balm *(Melissa officinalis)*
Also known as balm, lime balm, bee balm or melissa (the Greek word for honey bee). Lemon balm has been grown in the Mediterranean since

ancient times. The plants were used by bee keepers in the 17th and 18th centuries to keep their bees well behaved and close to the hives. The serrated, slightly hairy leaves look very much like small nettle leaves and in summer the plant is covered with tiny white flowers. The aroma can be quite overpowering in old, tough plants, especially those grown in pots. Lemon balm is wonderful for flavouring jellies, vinegar, vegetables, fresh fruits and cold drinks. In the 13th century, lemon balm was mixed with honey and used to make a tisane. It was said to chase away dark thoughts, strengthen a stressed nervous system and, above all, to keep you young. Today, herbalists still use it to calm and soothe.

Lemon verbena *(Verbena typhilla)*
Native to South America, lemon verbena was brought to Europe in the 18th century by the Spaniards. It has strong, lance-shaped leaves with an intensely fresh lemon aroma, at its best when the flowers are on the verge of blooming. However, even in winter, the few remaining dried-out leaves left on a plant still retain a strong fragrance when crushed. Use lemon verbena in fish dishes and with duck. It can also be used to flavour deserts and the delicate pink flowers can be sprinkled over the top to reinforce the flavour. To help insomnia, make a tisane (herb tea) from crushed fresh leaves, and sip the strained liquid last thing at night.

Lemongrass *(Cymbopogan citratus)*
Grown in South-east Asia, Africa and South America. Lemongrass is used in curries, soups and stews and works well with chicken or seafood. Use the bottom 5 cm or so of the bulb, and peel off the outer couple of leaves. Either bruise the whole grass and remove it before serving, or cut it very finely, then mash even more finely with a mortar and pestle. The stalks can also be used as kebab sticks. Freeze what you don't use – it can be used straight from frozen. Lemongrass can be grown in a greenhouse, or outdoors if you live in a mild climate. It is widely available from Asian markets.

Long pepper *(Piper longum)*
Black, elongated pine cone shaped pepper about 1.5 cm long, tasting very similar to black pepper, with a hint of warm sweetness. Highly valued by the ancient Greeks and Romans, but now rarely available in the West. Sometimes available from Middle Eastern shops and from mail order sources.

Lovage *(Levisticum officinale)*
Native to southern Europe. Sometimes known as sea parsley (it grows wild on sea cliffs and coastlines), lovage has a strong celery scent, and is known for its 'meaty' protein flavour. When young, the leaves taste salty and lemony and are good in salads or with vegetable and bean casseroles. When the plant grows tall and the leaves become slightly bitter, use them just for stews. Like many herbs, lovage was grown in the earliest monastic physic gardens for medicinal purposes. It was thought to be good for digestive problems and to relieve stomach cramps. At one time it was thought to be an aphrodisiac – hence the name.

Mace (*see* Nutmeg)

Mahlab *(Prunus mahaleb)*
Oval, tan kernels of mahalab cherry. Dried and ground; used in Middle Eastern baking. Available from some Turkish and Middle Eastern shops or mail order sources.

Marigold *(Calendula officinalis)*
The botanical name of the pot marigold is from the Latin *calendae* meaning 'little clock', so called because it flowers all year round in its natural habitat in the Mediterranean. It opens at sunrise and closes at sunset. Its bright orange and yellow flowers look pretty in the garden and add flavour and colour to food. Fresh and dried petals have been added to the cooking pot since the Middle Ages hence the name 'pot marigold'. The flowers have a warm, peppery, salty taste and work wonders with feta cheese and pine nuts. Teamed with ricotta in a stuffing for courgette flowers, they are sublime, and good in herb omelettes, too. The colour produced from the petals is the poor man's saffron, giving a wonderful orange tone with a subtle flavour, though not quite as spicily pungent as saffron. Calendula tincture has antiseptic properties.

Marjoram (*see* Sweet marjoram)

Mint *(Mentha)*
Mint was introduced to Europe by the Romans and has remained the most popular herb in the world. Peppermint tea of course is the drink of choice throughout the Middle East as it is as stimulating as coffee. It was said to restore and revive the spirit and to excite the appetite. Peppermint tea can also used to overcome nausea; infuse the leaves in boiling water for five minutes. Add to green tea as in Morocco, or use in iced mint tea, made by adding a handful of bruised mint leaves to a pot of Chinese green tea with the juice of a lime and some honey. Chill well, adding ice cubes, if you like. Another great summer drink is mint julep – mash mint leaves with sugar and mix with crushed ice and bourbon. **Thai mint** is very fragrant small leafed variety, with a hottish taste with a round hairless leaf and, when mature, has a dark red stem. Known as *bai sarae nae* in Thai, it is often available from Thai stores and it is also easy to propagate. Just put a stem into a glass of water until little roots show, then plant it in a pot. This is best done in spring from a bunch bought in a shop with a high turnover. This variety of mint is used quite extensively throughout South-east Asia, particularly in salads.

Spearmint *(M. spicata)*, or garden mint, is used in classic mint sauce with roast lamb. The perfect mint sauce is made by pouring boiling water over a handful of chopped mint with sugar. Let cool, then add cider vinegar to taste and serve with a silver or non-reactive spoon. Mint is also a favourite in kebabs, the comfort food of the Middle East, the raita of India and the sauce *paloise* of France.

Applemint *(M. suaveolens)* has soft grey-green fleshy leaves with a wonderful applemint aroma and flavour. Use whole sprigs when cooking peas, potatoes and beans.

Mustard *(Brassica juncea, B. nigra, B. hirta* or *Sinapsis alba)*
Native to Europe and Asia. The first species is brown, the second black, the third yellow. The round seeds are used whole as a pickling spice or fried in hot oil to flavour savoury dishes in India. Mustard is best known as a pungently hot condiment with a nose-searing kick – the seeds are crushed to a paste or dried and powdered, then mixed with liquid.

Nasturtium *(Tropaeolum majus)*
Native to South America. This flower was introduced into Spain from Peru by the conquistadors in the 16th century and its usage spread throughout Europe during the next century or so. Nasturtium is a relative of watercress and is also known as Indian cress. Nasturtium flowers and leaves have an intense, pungent, mustardy, peppery flavour. The flamboyant yellow, orange and red of the flowers make them the ideal spicy snap for many recipes, including sandwiches and salads – and they look beautiful, too.

Nigella *(Nigella sativa)*
Native to West Asia and southern Europe. The small aromatic black seeds are often mistakenly called onion seeds, although they have nothing to do with onions. Nigella has a most pleasant flavour when cooked, sharp but warm. It is known as *kalonji* in India, where it is widely used to flavour vegetable and bean dishes, added to naan bread or used in spice mixes. Nigella is also enjoyed in the Middle East and in parts of Africa. Available from Indian, Pakistani and Bangladeshi shops and some African and Middle Eastern shops.

Nutmeg *(Myristica fragrans)*
Native to Malaku (the Spice Islands) in Indonesia. Nutmeg's botanical name provides a clue to why this spice has always been treasured throughout the world. A highly fragrant brown nut housed within an outer shell, it is best freshly grated. Used in puddings, baking and in perfumed savoury dishes of the Middle East and Asia; it is a perfect partner for spinach and cream. The red, orange or yellow tendril-like case which covers the outer shell of the nutmeg is known as mace. Although close in flavour and scent, mace is more refined than nutmeg and is highly desirable for all manner of sweet and savoury dishes. For the best flavour, grind from the whole spice – sometimes called 'blades'. Available from Indian, Pakistani and Bangladeshi and Middle Eastern shops and delicatessens.

Oregano *(Origanum vulgare)*
Native to the Mediterranean. Also known as wild marjoram, oregano is a woody perennial, and the hotter the sun, the stronger the flavour. This genus belongs to the mint family. Italians use the flower heads just before they bloom as well as the leaves to flavour dishes. The many wild species of oregano are known collectively as 'rigani', which grows wild on hillsides and mountains throughout Greece. It's the wild species (not grown commercially) which is harvested when in bud and dried for maximum aroma. In Latin America and the Mediterranean, oregano is used much as parsley is used in Europe and North America. It is an essential ingredient in Italian cooking and a favourite herb in Greek cuisine – where would they be without it for tomato sauces and salads?

Pandan *(Pandanus odoratissimus)*
Also known as screwpine leaves, pandan is used to flavour and wrap food in much of South-east Asia. The long, fresh, green leaves are found in most Asian stores and they keep for weeks if they are wrapped in a plastic bag and stored in the salad drawer of the refrigerator. Bruise the leaves before using as a flavouring. It's quite floral and sweet, ideal for adding to sweet rice dishes, pancakes and curries. Extract the juice from the leaves and use it as a bright green food colouring; it is lovely in dishes such as coconut rice pudding or pancakes.

Paprika (*see* Chilli)

Parsley *(Petroselinum crispum)*
Native to the eastern Mediterranean, parsley was brought to western Europe in the 16th century where it began to grow so naturally and happily in rough places that it became known as 'rock celery'. The Greeks considered parsley to have too many associations with the devil, so preferred to keep its use to the medicine cabinet. The Romans, however, were happy to cook with it and it's now considered the most indispensable culinary herb. Flat leaf parsley (or French, Italian or Continental parsley, as it's often called) is essential to many traditional flavouring mixtures, such as Italian gremolata – a mix of parsley, chopped garlic and lemon zest, which is sprinkled over finished dishes. The French version is *persillade*, traditionally made without lemon. It is also used in *beurre de gascogne* – lots of blanched garlic and freshly chopped parsley mixed with duck or goose fat and mixed into a simple cassoulet at the last moment – and salmoriglio – a mixture of salt, garlic, lemon juice, olive oil and parsley, which is fabulous for sardines and fresh anchovies. Parsley (and mint) is also the essential herb in tabbouleh where classically the herbs are the dish and the grains of bulghur wheat are included simply to stop the juices from the other ingredients falling to the bottom of the bowl. Curly leaf parsley isn't the most fashionable herb and many discount it, but the flavour, when well grown, is iron-laden and sweet. It also holds up well to cooking in stuffing, but must be finely chopped, or the texture can be prickly. If you grow it at home, make sure the leaves are picked when tender. Like other parsley varieties, it contains masses of chlorophyll, the bright-green leaf juice which is packed with goodness.

Pepper *(Piper nigrum)*
Native to South-west India. Black pepper is perhaps the most widely used spice in the world, valued as an aromatic hot seasoning. The small, round berries grow on vines: picked just before they ripen, they are often sold in brine or dried and occasionally sold fresh. When dried in the sun they turn black; white peppercorns have had their outer skins removed. Green peppercorns are picked while still unripe and dried and or bottled. Pink peppercorns, often seen in mixed peppercorn packs, are from an unrelated plant, the Brazilian pepper tree *(Schinus terebinthifolius)*.

Pimentón (*see* Chilli)

Poppy seed *(Papaver somniferum)*
Native to the Mediterranean region and Middle East. Tiny round white, brown and black seeds used in breads and pastries, but further east in warming milk-based drinks or in sauces. Black seeds are most familiar in the West; white are common elsewhere.

Rosemary *(Rosmarinus officinalis)*
Native to the Mediterranean. Rosemary has been a culinary and medicinal herb since ancient Greek and Roman times. The Romans thought so highly of it they dedicated it to Venus, the Goddess of Love. It is also thought to improve the memory – as Ophelia said so sadly in Shakespeare's Hamlet, 'rosemary is for remembrance'. Apart from the classic partnerships with roast lamb or monkfish, the leaves are also capable of delivering some delicious flavours to puddings. Put the flowers or leaves in a pot of sugar for two weeks and use to make meringue or syrups, or warm the leaves and flowers with honey to pour over grilled figs, melon or orange salad.

Saffron *(Crocus sativus)*
Native to Persia and the Middle East. Saffron is the most expensive spice in the world, because the stigmas of the saffron crocus have to be hand-picked. Celebrated for its singular perfume and for the golden colour it brings to sweet and savoury dishes. The bright red stigmas ('threads' or 'strands') are usually infused in a little warm liquid before being added to a dish. Saffron's exquisite flavour graces rice dishes from Italy and Spain to the Middle East and South Asia; valued everywhere in puddings.

Sage *(Salvia officinalis)*
Native to the Mediterranean. From the Latin word *salvere* meaning 'to save', sage was – and still is – a highly valued medicinal herb, as well as a prime candidate for the award for one of the best culinary herbs. It is known as the 'herb

of the heart' and – even more astonishing – chewing the leaves is said to make teeth white and shiny. Sage is a popular herb in many regions of Italy. Its pungent robustness adds a new dimension to many dishes, including sage butter served with ravioli and gnocchi in Tuscany. In Germany, sage is cooked with eel, helping the digestive system cope with the richness of the dish. It makes a delicious flavouring for apple jelly to serve with pork, rich potato dishes with cream are transformed, while the flowers can be used to flavour bread dough, or to decorate the top of the loaf. Like many woody herbs, sage can stand up to long, slow cooking without losing its strength. In spring, sage has a gentle, mild aroma, but by the summer, when the flowers are just in bud, its volatile oils have matured in the heat of the sun. This is the combination that can create the 'medicine cabinet' effect that is too overpowering for food, unless used with a delicate hand. To care for sage, put bunches of leaves in a jug of shallow water with just the very ends of the stalks in the water, then put a plastic bag over the top and when the leaves have perked up take the bag off and leave the jug of herbs on the kitchen table as an edible decoration. If kept in the refrigerator, the leaves will turn limp and sad.

Purple sage *(S. o.* 'Purpurascens'*)* can be used as common sage, but it is not as pungent, so it is good pan-fried, or dipped in batter and deep-fried.

Pineapple sage *(S. elegans* 'Scarlet Pineapple'*)* has red-edged, pointed, oval leaves with red stems and scarlet flowers in winter. Early in the season the leaves have a strong pineapple flavour when crushed. This flavour diminishes after flowering. There are many scented sages you can plant in your garden, and they are worth some experimentation as culinary ammunition.

Salep/Sahlab *(Orchis mascula)*

The root of a ground orchid, used as a thickener, but contributes its mild flavour to milky drinks in the Middle East; it can also be used in puddings. It can be difficult to find, but it is sometimes available from Middle Eastern shops.

Sansho *(Zanthoxylum* spp.*)*

Native to the far East. A close relative of Szechuan pepper, sansho is a berry from the Japanese prickly ash tree, which is dried and ground to a powder. It has a tangy flavour and is used to sprinkle over foods. Available from some health food stores, Japanese shops and by mail order.

Savory *(Satureja)*

Introduced into northern Europe by the Romans, who used this highly aromatic herb as a peppery, spicy flavouring. It was commonly used to ease digestion after the enjoyment of certain challenging foods and, as if that weren't enough, it was also considered an aphrodisiac.

Summer savory *(S. hortensis)* is an annual and is known as the bean herb because it eases flatulence. The flavour of the tender leaves is similar to thyme. Both the leaves and flowers – white or pale pink – can be used with beans, lentils, char-grilled fish and vegetables.

Winter savory *(S. montana)* is evergreen, with lilac or white flowers, and a little stronger and a bit more resinous than summer savory with a flavour similar to thyme. It suits bean dishes as well as char-grilled meat and fish. A commercially grown savory is now available from supermarkets but it hasn't the same strength as homegrown.

Sesame *(Sesamum indicum)*

Native to East Africa and South Asia. Small white, brown, or black seeds with a nutty flavour, emphasized by toasting. Appreciated for their texture in Japan and China; in the Middle East and eastern Mediterranean they are crushed to make tahini paste and sweet halva; the white variety is used throughout the world to coat snacks and bagels.

Star anise *(Illicium verum)*

Native to China and Vietnam. A beautiful, brown, star-shaped spice with a strong, perfumed anise scent and flavour. In its ground form, it permeates Chinese five-spice mixture. When used whole – or broken into 'petals' – it flavours soups, sauces, cooking liquids and marinades. Available from Chinese shops.

Sumac *(Rhus coriaria)*

Reddish-brown berries, dried and used as a souring agent throughout the Middle East. The ground spice is sprinkled over grilled meats and fish and used in the Middle Eastern spice mixture Zahtar (page 174). Available from Middle Eastern shops.

Sweet cicely *(Myrrhis odorata)*

Native to northern Europe. Sometimes known as liquorice root. This is a herb you must grow yourself, because as yet no one sells it by the bunch, which is a shame as its qualities demand that it should be in more prominent use. Its firm, chervil-like leaves and froth of white flowers have a sweet anise and liquorice flavour, so it tastes very good in all things sweet. It loves the companionship of sharp fruits in dishes like crumbles, reducing the acidity, so you need less sugar. Add the leaves to vegetable soups right at the end of cooking to sweeten and bring out their flavour. The leaves can also be used in green salads and with grilled goats' cheese. The leaves and flowers also make fantastic tempura with extra leaves infused in a syrup, then strained to use as a dip.

Sweet marjoram *(Origanum majorana)*

Introduced to Europe in the Middle Ages from North Africa, marjoram is now found all over the Mediterranean and western Asia. Use in dishes that don't need lengthy cooking, such as soufflés and light food. The leaves become floppy quickly, so add to salads at the last minute. Marjoram's generic name is 'oregano', while confusingly oregano's other name is 'wild marjoram'. Sweet marjoram looks delicate with light-green, soft leaves and a beige–pink stalk. The leaves are sweetly scented, with white or pinky-purple flowers. It has a more fleshy and tender look to it than its stronger looking relative, pot marjoram (see below). The antiseptic qualities for which this genus was famous meant that it was used as a strewing herb, scattered around kitchens to keep them sweet-smelling. As a result, it was a prominent crop in the kitchen gardens of Renaissance times.

Pot marjoram *(O. onites)* looks very similar to oregano, except the leaves are a lighter green and the flowers tend to be paler. It is also known as French marjoram. It has a slightly tougher leaf than sweet marjoram, and so it can be used more robustly in tomato sauces and dishes that are cooked a little longer.

Golden marjoram *(O. vulgare* 'Aureum'*)* has a very soft, pale, greeny-gold leaf with white flowers. The flavour is excellent and stands up well to cooking when added ten minutes before the end.

Szechuan pepper *(Zanthoxylum piperitum)*

Native to China. Also known as fagara. Brick-red berry with inner seeds from the prickly ash tree; best toasted before being used. Szechuan pepper is a key component of Chinese five-spice mixture; also used in spiced salt seasoning. Has woody-peppery flavour and a slight numbing effect. Sold in Chinese shops.

Tamarind *(Tamarindus indica)*

Native to Africa and probably South Asia. Brown,

lumpy, bean-like pod is usually sold in blocks, to be soaked in water, squeezed and strained to make tamarind water or concentrate. Tamarind adds a delicious sour tang to savoury dishes. It is popular in the Middle East and Asia and makes a refreshing drink in parts of the Caribbean. Available from South-east Asian, Indian, Pakistani, Bangladeshi and Middle Eastern shops. Also sold as ready-made concentrate.

Tansy *(Tanacetum vulgare)*
Native to Europe, the Greeks and Romans considered tansy a symbol of immortality. It is very deep in flavour and quite unforgettable. Tansy was the name of the herb as well as the name of the pudding it flavoured – eaten at Easter time, often in the form of bread-like cakes. At other times it appeared in rich mousse-like creamy puddings. Rubbed on lamb it gives a similar flavour to rosemary. In the 17th century it was stir-fried with oranges and sugar.
Tansy has strong antiseptic qualities and before there was such a thing as refrigeration, it was used to wrap meat to repel flies. Like many bitter herbs, it has a reputation as a digestive stimulant – people with a sensitive constitution may like to substitute bay or thyme instead.

Tarragon *(Artemesia dracunculus)*
Native to southern Russia. Tarragon is the aristocrat of the herb garden. The aromatic, shiny, smooth, light-green leaves are the only soft leaf herb that can withstand long cooking, which helps to mellow the flavour, losing the harsher side of its character. This herb makes famous pairings with chicken or rich cream sauces. The pungent, bossy, anise flavour turns saintly and mellow after 30 minutes in the oven with chicken pieces, white wine and double cream. Remove the branch of tarragon towards the end of cooking and add a second hit of it about five minutes before the end of the cooking time. The flavour of tarragon is at its most pungent in high summer. It can have a numbing effect on the tongue when chewed raw, and is quite alcoholic in flavour – like pastis, but without the water to temper its strength. Many gardeners have been disappointed when they discover they have the tasteless Russian variety, rather than the glorious French one. Take care when you buy small plants – scratch and sniff the leaves to make sure. Tarragon is one of those herbs that survives the drying process. French roast chicken with dried tarragon is delicious – the version in which many people first taste this wonderful herb.

Thyme *(Thymus vulgaris)*
Native to southern Europe. From the Greek *thymos*, meaning 'to perfume', thyme has so many varieties, which are all full of character and all with their own subtle aroma and flavour. The ancient Egyptians and Greeks knew the powerful antiseptic and preservative qualities of thyme and its ability to stimulate the brain and improve the memory. Roman cooks used it to preserve their meat as its strong antiseptic qualities delayed spoiling. In the 17th century, cooking with thyme was believed to make fairies visible. Today it is mainly used in stews, sauces and with grilled or roasted meats. Broad-leaved thyme *(T. pulgegiodes)* can be used instead of common thyme.

Lemon thyme ***(T. x citriodorus)*** tastes strongly of citrus and is delicious grilled with peaches and figs or stuffed inside a fish. Add a few sprigs to a marinade for lamb along with oil and black pepper, then let chill in the refrigerator for 24 hours, adding salt for the last 30 minutes as you let the lamb return to room temperature before cooking.

Triffla/Tirphal *(Zanthoxylum rhetsa)*
A black berry which only grows in Western India, with a woody, slightly bitter flavour, triffla is related to Szechuan pepper and sansho. The bitter seeds are discarded and the berry is usually toasted before use. Difficult to find outside India.

Turmeric *(Curcuma longa)*
Native to South-east Asia. A brown rhizome with bright orange flesh and a member of the ginger family. Turmeric is mostly available in ground form in the West, but it is also used fresh throughout Asia and the Middle East. Aromatic, peppery and musky, it is used to spice oil and is used in curry pastes and powders. It is also a strong dye, giving a golden colour to anything it touches.

Vanilla *(Vanilla planifolia)*
Native to Central America. The cured, long, dark brown pods are fragrant, with naturally occurring crystals of vanillin which provide scent and flavour. Good-quality vanilla is expensive. The pods may be used whole to flavour sauces or the poaching liquid for fruits; if split, the seeds can be scraped out and incorporated into puddings and ice cream. Also available as pure vanilla extract, or the more concentrated essence. Synthetic vanilla flavouring is a common but very inferior product.

Vietnamese balm *(Elsholtzia ciliata)*
Grown and used in the West. Although not from the same family as lemon balm, it has similar attributes and could be used as a substitute.

Vietnamese coriander *(Polygonum odoratum)*
Often known as rau rau, laksa leaf and Vietnamese mint, Vietnamese coriander is fast becoming *the* Asian herb. Its refreshing flavour has a hot, citrusy note and the coriander-style pungency stands up well to cooking. It can be added halfway through cooking or wilted in just before serving. You can also scatter it over the dish, to serve. The long pointed leaf has an aubergine-coloured horseshoe shape in the centre, making it a very attractive addition to the ubiquitous Vietnamese table salads, served with every Vietnamese meal. You can also deep-fry the leaves. The plants can be bought from nurseries and the cut stems are available from Asian stores. Its native habitat is on the banks of streams so prefers its roots to be kept moist. Its stems are succulent, which is a sign of a water-loving plant.

Violet *(Viola tricolor)*
Native to Europe, violet is also known as wild pansy, heartsease or Johnny jump-up. The common name 'pansy' is from the French word *pensée*, meaning a thought or remembrance of love. Although you shouldn't eat too many at once, they are good in salads, in stuffing or crystallized and used to decorate puddings. An infusion made from violet flowers was said to mend a broken heart.

Sweet violets ***(V. odorata)*** are the purple violets classically used to flavour violet cream chocolates.

Wasabi *(Wasabia japonica)*
Native to Japan; the root of the mountain hollyhock. Wasabi is often called Japanese horseradish because of the similar, very hot kick. It is an indispensable sushi condiment. Used freshly grated or as a paste in Japan, it is available in the West as a powder or a ready-made paste from Japanese shops and in some supermarkets and Chinese shops.

mail order and shops

HERBS, PLANTS & SEEDS

4°C
1 Spital House
New Spitalfields Market
Leyton
London E10 5SQ
(020) 8558 9708
www.4degreesc.co.uk
Supplies top London restaurants, has a refrigerated warehouse in Britain's busiest wholesale market, scores of products grown exclusively for it.

Arne Herbs
Limeburn Nurseries
Limeburn Hill
Chew Magna
Bristol BS40 8QW
(01275) 333399
www.arneherbs.co.uk
Suppliers of traditional, medicinal, Renaissance, medieval, Tudor and rare plants and seeds worldwide. Wild flower conservation. Rare and culinary herbs.

Chesters Walled Garden
Chollerford
Hexham
Northumberland NE46 4BQ
(01434) 681483
Email: enquiries@chesterswalled garden.co.uk
www.chesterswalledgarden.co.uk
No catalogue: no mail order, but seeds sold from their shop. Situated next to Chesters Roman Fort, on the line of Hadrian's Wall. National collection of thymes and marjorams and includes a Roman garden. Opening times: 10 am–5 pm daily, 1 April to 31 October. Opening times from November to end of March depend on the weather (phone first).

Cool Chile Co.
Unit 7, Buspace Studios
Conlan Street
London W10 5AP
(0870) 902 1145
Email: dodie@coolchile.co.uk
www.coolchile.co.uk
A wide selection of dried chillies and seeds, including epazote and achiote (annatto) seeds. Also stocks Mexican goods, such as tortillas.

English Cottage Garden Nursery
Eggarton Cottages
Eggarton Lane
Godmersham
Kent CT4 7DY
(01227) 730242
Email: enquiries@englishplants.co.uk
www.englishplants.co.uk
A small nursery growing traditional cottage garden plants, wildflowers and herbs. Situated in Kent, on the edge of Romney Marsh, beside the Royal Military Canal. Visiting by appointment only. All plants grown in peat-free, coir compost.

Foxhollow Nurseries
73 Lower Pillory Downs
Little Woodcoat Estate
Carshalton
Surrey SM5 4DD
(020) 8660 0991

Iden Croft Herbs
International Herb Centre of Kent
Frittenden Road
Staplehurst
Kent TN12 0DH
(01580) 891 432
www.herbs-uk.com
Established over 30 years in the grounds of a former Augustinian Friary. The walled garden is Tudor. Later, the land formed part of the Staplehurst Manor estate. The kitchen gardens, orchard, hot houses etc. were on the area which now form Iden Croft Herbs.

Jekka's Herb Farm
Rose Cottage
Shellards Lane,
Alveston
Bristol BS35 3SY
(01454) 418878
Email: farm@jekkasherbfarm.co.uk
www.jekkasherbfarm.com
Catalogue available on request. The farm holds 8 open days per year, but is not open to the public on a daily basis.

Laurel Farm Herbs
Main Road
A12 Kelsale
Saxmundham
Suffolk IP17 2RG
(01728) 668223
Email: chris@laurelfarmherbs.co.uk
www.laurelfarmherbs.co.uk
Growing herbs delivered to your door.

Marshalls Seeds
S.E. Marshalls & Co.
Alconbury Hill
Huntingdon
Cambs PE28 4HY
(01480) 443391
www.marshalls-seeds.co.uk
Mail order. All you need for the kitchen garden: vegetable plants, fruit, seeds and gardening products.

The Organic Gardening Catalogue
Riverdene Business Park
Molesey Road
Hersham
Surrey KT12 4RG
(0845) 130 1304
www.organiccatalog.com
Mail order organic seeds including herbs, salads and fruit.

Simpson's Seeds
The Walled Garden Nursery
Horningsham
Warminster
Wiltshire BA12 7NQ
(01985) 845004
Email: sales@simpsonseeds.co.uk
www.simpsonsseeds.co.uk
Seeds and plantlets, including salad vegetables and chillies.

Suffolk Herbs
Monks Farm
Kelvedon
Colchester
Essex CO5 9PG
(01376) 572456
www.suffolkherbs.com
Mail order herbs, salad vegetables and organic seeds.

NATURAL PEST CONTROL

The Green Gardener
1 Whitmore Wood
Rendlesham
Suffolk IP12 2US
(01394) 420087
Email: jon@greengardener.co.uk
www.greengardener.co.uk
Mail order source for ladybirds, lacewings and natural forms of pest control. Includes wormeries, worms for the garden, home composting, wildlife homes and feeders, biological control of slugs, vine weevil, aphids – leatherjackets, chafer grubs, whitefly and encarsia.

MAIL ORDER

Cool Chile Co.
Dried chillies and Mexican goods. *See under Herbs, Plants & Seeds.*

Greencades
142 High Street
Deal
Kent CT14 6BE
(01304) 362188
www.greencades.co.uk
Shop and mail order company: useful for unusual spices and herbs.

Peppers by Post
Sea Spring Farm
West Bexington

Dorchester
Dorset DT2 9DD
(01308) 897766
Email: info@peppersbypost.biz
www.peppersbypost.biz
Mail order company for a range of fresh, home-grown chillies in season (July–December).

Seasoned Pioneers
Unit 8, Stadium Court
Stadium Road
Plantation Business Park
Bromborough
Wirral CH62 3RP
(0800) 068 2348/(0151) 343 1122
www.seasonedpioneers.co.uk
Email: feedback@seasoned pioneers.co.uk
Mail order for over 100 different mixes and spices, including unusual spices.

Selfridges Food Hall
Selfridges
400 Oxford Street
London W1A 1AB
(08708) 377377
www.selfridges.com
Gourmet and international ingredients. Food halls also in Manchester and Birmingham stores. Mail order available.

The Spice Shop
1 Blenheim Crescent
London W11 2EE
(020) 7221 4448
Email: enquiries@thespiceshop.co.uk
www.thespiceshop.co.uk

TK Trading
Unit 7, The Chase Centre
8 Chase Road
Park Royal
London NW10 6QD
(020) 8453 1743
www.japan-foods.co.uk
(in Japanese)
Email: tktrade@uk2.so-net.com
Japanese food specialists.

SPECIALIST SHOPS

Atari-Ya (Japanese)
7 Station Parade
Noel Road
London W3 ODS
(020) 8896 1552
Japanese shiso leaves and sahimi-quality seafood

Madhav's (Indian)
59, Lower Cathedral Road
Cardiff
South Glamorgan
CF11 6LW
(02920) 372947

Paya Thai (Thai)
101–103 Kew Road
Richmond TW9 2PN
(020) 8332 2959
www.payathai.co.uk

Sri Thai (Thai)
56 Shepherd's Bush Road
London W6 7PH
(020) 7602 0621

Super Bahar (Iranian and Middle Eastern)
349 Kensington High Street
London W8 6NW
(020) 7603 5083

Talad Thai (Thai and South-east Asian)
320 Upper Richmond Road
London SW15 6TL
(020) 8789 8084

Thanh Xuân Supermarket (Vietnamese)
84 Deptford High Street
London SE8 4RG
(020) 8691 8106

Tawana Oriental Supermarket (South-east Asian)
18 Chepstow Road
London W2 5BD
(020) 7221 6316
also at
243–245 Plaistow Road
London E15 3EU
(020) 8503 1639
www.tawana.co.uk

ASIAN SPECIALIST FOOD DISTRICTS

Southall; Tooting; and Ealing Road, Wembley
Three areas in London full of Indian, Bangladeshi and Pakistani grocers and shops, stocking a wide range of South Asian spices and ingredients.

Edgware Road, London
Lebanese and Middle Eastern spices and ingredients.

Gerrard Street area, Soho, London
Chinese, Japanese, South-east Asian stores.

picture credits

All photographs by **Peter Cassidy** except:

William Lingwood
Pages 1, 164–165, 170

Nicki Dowey
Pages 62–63

Philip Webb
Pages 140–141

recipe credits

Manisha Gambhir Harkins
Pages 16, 19, 20, 23, 24, 31, 35, 36, 51, 52, 59, 60, 64, 75, 79, 81, 82, 89, 90, 94, 97, 102, 114, 117, 131, 132, 135, 154, 156, 159, 160, 163, 166, 167

Linda Tubby
Pages 12, 15, 27, 28, 32, 41, 42, 45, 46, 49, 55, 56, 67, 68, 71, 72, 76, 84, 87, 93, 98, 101, 107, 108, 111, 112, 123, 124, 127, 128, 136, 139, 143, 144, 147, 148, 151, 153, 168, 169, 170, 171, 172–179

Vatcharin Bhumichitr
Page 118

index